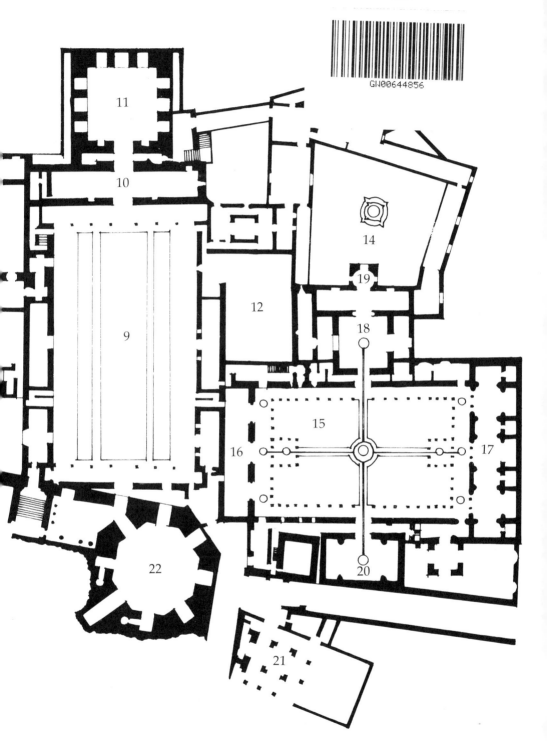

The Alhambra

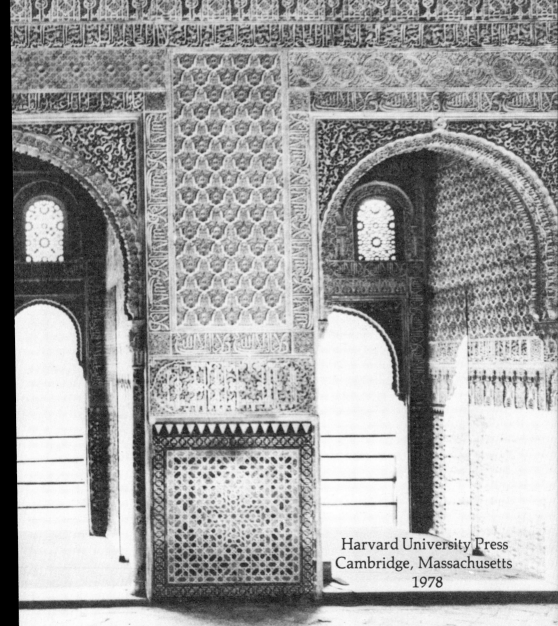

THE ALHAMBRA

Oleg Grabar

Harvard University Press
Cambridge, Massachusetts
1978

Library of Congress Cataloging in Publication Data
Grabar, Oleg.
  The Alhambra.
  Bibliography: p.
  Includes index.
  1. Alhambra. I. Title.
NA387.G73   728.8′2′094682   77-24555
ISBN 0-674-01556-8

Designed by Gerald Cinamon

TO TERRY

CONTENTS

LIST OF ILLUSTRATIONS

21. The Court of the Myrtles, south façade (Foto Mas, Barcelona).
22. The Court of the Myrtles, north façade (Douglas Dickins, F.R.P.S., London).
23. The Court of the Myrtles, north gallery (A. F. Kersting, London).
24. The Court of the Myrtles, wall decoration in the north gallery (Gerald Cinamon, London).
25. The Court of the Myrtles, niche at the end of the north gallery (Ronald Sheridan, London).
26. The Court of the Myrtles, detail of the same niche (Douglas Dickins, F.R.P.S., London).
27. The Court of the Myrtles, niche between the north gallery and the Sala de la Barca (Gerald Cinamon, London).
28. The Sala de la Barca, corner detail showing the wooden ceiling (Gerald Cinamon, London).
29. The Hall of the Ambassadors, section (Goury–Jones, *Plans, Elevations, Sections, and Details of the Alhambra*, O. Jones, London, 1842–5).
30. The Hall of the Ambassadors, exterior (Foto Mas, Barcelona).
31. The Hall of the Ambassadors, interior (Ronald Sheridan, London).
32. The Hall of the Ambassadors, interior (A. F. Kersting, London).
33. The Hall of the Ambassadors, ceiling (Foto Mas, Barcelona).
34. The Hall of the Ambassadors, central northern alcove (Alinari, Florence).
35. The Hall of the Ambassadors, detail of the central northern alcove (Gerald Cinamon, London).
36. The bath, section and plan (Goury–Jones).
37. The bath, main hall, Sala de las Camas (Foto Mas, Barcelona).
38. The Court of the Lions, from the air, looking east (Foto Mas, Barcelona).
39. The Court of the Lions, looking north-east (Douglas Dickins, F.R.P.S., London).
40. The Court of the Lions, section (Goury–Jones).
41. The Court of the Lions, section (Goury–Jones).
42. The Court of the Lions, looking west (Douglas Dickins, F.R.P.S., London).
43. The Hall of the Kings, ceiling of square unit (*Ars Hispaniae*, Vol. IV).
44. The Hall of the Kings (Alinari, Florence).
45. The Hall of the Kings (A. F. Kersting, London).
46. The Hall of the Kings, alcove, ceiling painting (Foto Mas, Barcelona).
47. The Hall of the Kings, alcove, detail of ceiling painting (Adam Woolfitt, Susan Griggs Agency, London).
48. The Hall of the Kings, alcove, detail of ceiling painting (Adam Woolfitt, Susan Griggs Agency, London).

PREFACE

The idea for this book was given to me by John Fleming and Hugh Honour. Although they should not bear any responsibility for its shortcomings, I am grateful to them for having compelled me to focus around an acknowledged masterpiece of Islamic architecture thoughts and ideas about secular architecture and Islamic architectural aesthetics which were until then rather disorganized. To some readers these ideas may still be too tentative and unclear, in as much as I have little claim to be fully competent with western Islamic culture. But they will have fulfilled their purpose if they inspire or irritate others to come up with alternative ones.

As usual, many people have helped in the writing of this book: John Fleming and Hugh Honour with much editorial help; Susan Rose-Smith with cheerful hunting for photographs; Avril Lamb and Meredith Spencer with typing and occasional library research; Renata Holod with important criticism of contents; and especially Frederick Bargebuhr, whose inspiring work on the Alhambra led me to think about this monument, even though some of my interpretations are different from his. My debt to all of them is immense.

One last word of partial apology is in order. Transliterations from Arabic have been simplified, as a book for the general public does not need precise philological symbols.

INTRODUCTION

One may as well begin with Washington Irving's account of the fall of Granada and the taking of the Alhambra in 1492, when Queen Isabella was already backing Columbus in his great adventure. Ferdinand and Isabella arrived there on 6 January, the day of Epiphany, of that fateful year. Most of the Muslim army and household had left the Alhambra a few days earlier, and only Abu Abdallah, the Boabdil of Washington Irving's story and the last Arab ruler in Andalusia, remained with a small retinue. While the victorious King and Queen with most of their army were waiting in the valley below, a small Christian detachment climbed up the hill of the Alhambra to take formal possession.

At length they [Ferdinand and Isabella] saw the silver cross, the great standard of this crusade, elevated on the Torre de la Vela, or great watch-tower, and sparkling in the sunbeams. . . Beside it was planted the pennon of the glorious apostle St James; and a great shout of 'Santiago! Santiago!' rose throughout the army. Lastly was reared the royal standard, by the knight of arms, with the shout of 'Castile, Castile! For King Ferdinand and Queen Isabella.' The words were echoed by the whole army. . . At sight of these signals of possession, the sovereigns fell upon their knees, giving thanks to God for this great triumph. The whole assembled host followed their example; and the choristers of the royal chapel broke forth into the solemn anthem of *Te Deum laudamus*.

Then the sovereigns proceeded to the Alhambra. On their way they met Boabdil leaving with a small band of followers. The defeated prince saluted the victorious King and Queen, took delivery of his son, who had been kept as a hostage by the Christians, and gave up the keys of the city. Then

the unfortunate Boabdil continued on. . .that he might not behold the entrance of the Christians into his capital. His devoted band of cavaliers followed him in gloomy silence; but heavy sighs burst from their bosoms, as shouts of joy and strains of triumphant music were borne on the breeze from the victorious army.

As he took a last glance at his city, he cried and, while his mother's alleged statement that 'you do well to weep like a woman for what you failed to defend like a man' merely added insult to injury, the place is still known as the 'hill of the last sigh of the Moor' [Silla del Mauro]. In the meantime, the Spanish court had ascended to the palace of the Alhambra and entered by the great Gate of Justice.

The halls, lately occupied by turbaned infidels, now rustled with stately dames and Christian courtiers, who wandered with eager curiosity over this far-famed palace, admiring its verdant courts and gushing fountains, its halls decorated with elegant arabesques, and storied with inscriptions, and the splendour of its gilded and brilliantly painted ceilings.[1]

It is through this sort of dramatic account that the Alhambra penetrated into romantic and popular imagination as Spain became the most accessible country to French literati or English aristocrats in search of the picturesque. Shortly before Washington Irving's *Chronicle of the Conquest of Granada* (1829) and *Legends of the Alhambra* (1832), Chateaubriand had recounted the legendary loves and tragic battles of *The Last of the Abencerrajes* (1826). In Victor Hugo's *Les Orientales* (1829) and in some of Théophile Gautier's more inspired pages of verse or of prose (1840 and later), the Alhambra and, by extension, Granada became simultaneously symbols of sensuous exoticism and aesthetic ideals of beautiful form, an 'earthly paradise', as it was called by Gautier,[2] or a site of 'barbaric magnificence', according to Washington Irving.[3] In Spain itself a unique Romantic literary tradition became centred on the Alhambra and Granada. As described by its recent historian, Melchor Fernandez Almagro, it hovered uneasily between several incompatible poles: deeply felt national or regional emotions, genuine concern for the Muslim past, and 'oriental delirium'.[4]

A romanticism of another kind, searching for new doctrines and new ideas about the arts and especially about ornament, led Jules Goury, Owen Jones and Girault de Prangey to the Alhambra, also in the thirties and forties of the nineteenth century. It is interesting and distressing that theirs should still be the best available elevations and sections of architecture and drawings of decorative designs from the Alhambra.[5] Their models and designs, copied and studied in art schools all over the world, came to be interwoven with the romantic associations spun by Washington Irving, Chateaubriand and others and led to the innumerable hotels, bars, and movie houses called Granada or Alhambra. On more formal architectural thought their impact was far less impressive, although here and there, and as late as in some of Yamasaki's designs, one can detect the imprint of superficial and at times even profound aspects of the Alhambra's architecture.

The uniqueness of the achievements of Goury and Jones and Girault de Prangey does not mean that after 1850 no other work was done on the palace or that no thought was generated beyond the verbose panegyrics of guide books or luxury picture books. A considerable body of scholarly literature has in fact accumulated around the Alhambra – technical and archaeological studies, detailed surveys and descriptions and, more recently, several probing studies of the intellectual, aesthetic and historical contexts. The most important of these are listed and discussed in the bibliographical note (pp. 211–15).

This book is not an attempt to summarize all the literature. Nor is it an archaeological history or a new guide book. Years of investigations and excavations would be necessary before a true archaeological history of the monument could be written, and the existing Spanish guide books are adequate for most practical purposes. It seeks instead to explain the Alhambra in history, to provide or rather to suggest the reasons why this particular monument was put together when it was and to relate it to the traditions, both Islamic and non-Islamic, from which it derived. For, whatever its own formal or symbolic peculiarities may be, the Alhambra is the best-preserved palace from a civilization, the Islamic one, which was known throughout the Middle Ages for the uniquely luxurious art of its princes. But, in a broader sense, the Alhambra is one of the few well-preserved medieval palaces of any kind; between Diocletian's palace in Spalato and the Louvre or the Escorial, ruins and written descriptions are far more numerous than complete surviving examples. The main question I shall seek to answer is, therefore, that of the ways in which and the degree to which the Alhambra can legitimately be considered a characteristic monument of court art in Islam and by extension in the Middle Ages as a whole.

In order to set the building properly in this particular context of its meaning in history, it is necessary first of all to describe what remains of it and to define as precisely as possible its physical characteristics and the times to which it belongs. In this task, which occupies the first chapter of the book, little originality is claimed. Indeed, it is likely that in many archaeological details subsequent work may modify my conclusions. Similarly, as regards the history and culture generally of fourteenth-century Spain, much remains to be discovered. For the main parts of the building, however, and for the major events of the time there is, on the whole, agreement about the evidence.

The second chapter has two purposes: to identify from literary sources and internal evidence the living, ceremonial, or symbolic meanings and functions which can be attributed to the Alhambra, and at the same time to situate these meanings and functions in relation to other palaces and thus to define the importance of the Alhambra within the development of secular architecture in general. In large part this chapter is an essay in the iconography of architecture, a field which is notoriously fraught with methodological and intellectual pitfalls. It would be presumptuous to claim that all of them have been avoided, but the chapter's objective will be met if its hypotheses and conclusions are tested and modified by further research.

No investigation of the Alhambra can avoid a discussion of its visual form, for it is this, more than any historical or symbolic connotations, which attracts visitors from all countries and all walks of life, and it is about this that the most poetically laudatory or vehemently critical pages have been written. In Chapter 3, therefore, I shall try to define and evaluate its form, which poses in striking fashion not only some very general questions of aesthetic appreciation but also some highly practical ones about the relationship between construction, function, and ornament, for even though many of these have been the subject of contemporary debate, they are still mostly unresolved. All I shall be able to do is to propose an additional set of hypotheses, with the hope of enticing others to pursue these matters.

Throughout these chapters two concerns will be predominant: to understand a specific monument and to establish its historical and aesthetic value within a broader series of monuments. For, in the final analysis, the key question we shall have to answer is the degree of uniqueness which can be attributed to the Alhambra. Is this stunning creation by a second-rate dynasty in moribund Muslim Spain the accidentally preserved example of a relatively common type of monument, as would be, for instance, a Gothic cathedral, a Romanesque church, or a Renaissance palace or villa in France or Italy? Or is it an aesthetically and iconographically unique monument like Hagia Sophia or the Parthenon?

As these questions indicate, the pages which follow form an exploratory essay rather than an exhaustive archaeological and art-historical investigation. Its purpose is primarily to develop a number of possible interpretations of a celebrated building and secondarily to suggest avenues for further research, for, as with any masterpiece, there are many different ways of focusing on it. The Notes are limited to specific references without further elaboration, and the Bibliography contains only the most important studies and descriptions which may help others to pursue or modify the interpretations proposed here.

1. Aerial view of the Alhambra

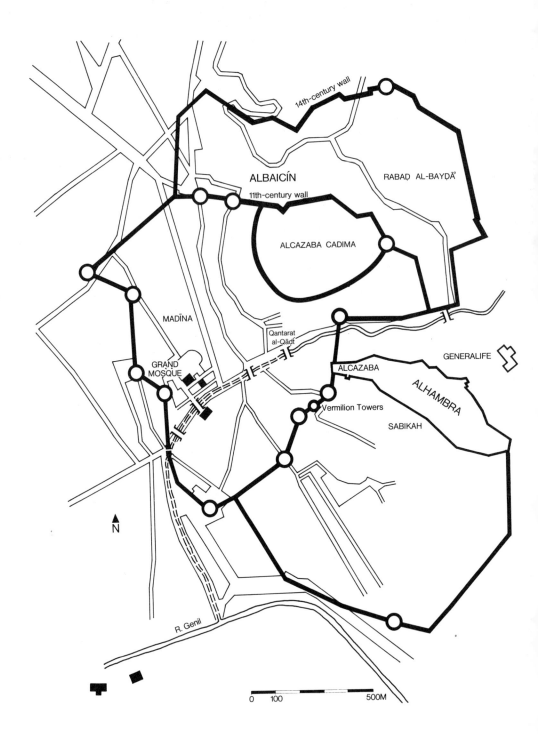

ALBAICÍN

RABAḌ AL-BAYḌĀ'

14th-century wall

11th-century wall

ALCAZABA CADIMA

MADÎNA

Qantarat al-Qāḍī

GRAND MOSQUE

GENERALIFE

ALCAZABA

ALHAMBRA

Vermilion Towers

SABIKAH

N

R. Genil

0   100   500M

2. *Plan of Nasrid Granada*

Chapter 1

THE
ARCHAEOLOGICAL
AND
HISTORICAL
SETTING

The Alhambra, whose name is an abbreviation of Qal'at al-Hamra, 'the red fort', probably because of the red clay of the surrounding terrain, is a fortified enclosure of irregular shape located on a hill known in medieval sources as the Sabikah [1 and 2]. The latter is one of several spurs overlooking from the east the Vega, the fertile upper part of the valley of the Genil and its tributaries, such as the Darro to the north-west of the Alhambra hill. These spurs are all extensions of the Sierra Nevada, the highest mountain chain of the Iberian peninsula, whose snow-capped summits surround Granada from the east and the south-east. The Sabikah differs from other such spurs in two ways. One is an advantage. It is the highest of the spurs in the immediate vicinity of Granada, and access to it from the north or the west is quite forbidding [3]. From the south-west and the south it is somewhat easier to reach; it is separated from the mountain to the south-east by a ravine, which is narrow and not very deep, but quite sufficient to transform the Sabikah into a superb natural position of defence [4 and 5]. The second peculiarity of this spur is a corollary of the first but a disadvantage. It is that, precisely because of the gully which separates it from the sierra, it could not easily be supplied with water. In order for it to be used for permanent living, cisterns or aqueducts were necessary, and both were vulnerable.

Although neither archaeological nor literary sources are very clear on the exact chronology of the early use of the Sabikah, it seems likely that two conditions were, jointly or separately, necessary for its growth into something more than a convenient but temporary refuge in times of danger. One is some major development beyond the hill itself – in the valley or on less isolated neighbouring hills – since the Sabikah alone does not lend itself to easy habitation. The second condition is that sufficient security and wealth must prevail in the region as a whole to allow for the monumental and technical transformation of this waterless spur in a forbidding mountain chain.

It is easy enough to observe by walking around the walls that the Alhambra is connected to a large number of extraneous features. To the north-west a wall follows down the steep contours of the terrain; in ways which have now disappeared, it joined somewhere the outer wall of the city in the plain. Nearby, over the Darro, stand the ruins of a bridge probably erroneously identified as the *jisr al-Qadi* known in texts but somehow

3. *The Alhambra from the west*

4. *The Vermilion Towers: watercolour by David Roberts*

involved with movements to and from the Alhambra. To the west a largely preserved wall leads from the Sabikah to the impressive complex known as the Torres Bermejas, the Vermilion Towers. What happened beyond this ensemble has been largely obliterated, but it seems that the handsome park which now occupies the gently sloping southern edge of the Sabikah and the large Carmen de los Martires to the south-east originally formed part of the Alhambra complex, even if it remained outside its walled enclosure. Finally, to the east traces remain of the aqueducts which brought water to the Sabikah, and beyond the ravine is a succession of superb medieval gardens and pavilions forming the Generalife, the gardens and palaces of the *dar al-'Arusah* (the House of the Bride) and of the Alixares. In other words, the Alhambra hill itself, which has been well described by Torres Balbás as an 'enormous boat anchored between the mountain

and the plain',[1] was not developed alone but in relationship to its surroundings, both the city below and the hills around. The key archaeological problem is the chronology of these developments. Did the life and needs of the Alhambra spread beyond the Sabikah? Or did developments elsewhere in the area make the Alhambra possible, or even perhaps necessary?

A partial answer is provided by the history of medieval Granada,[2] which is itself inseparable from the history of Islamic Spain. Although the first Arab incursions into Spain occurred as early as July 710, it was in the spring of 711 that the first substantial body of Muslims crossed the Straits of Gibraltar and began an infiltration of the Iberian peninsula and of southern France which led them all the way to Poitiers by 732. The battle which took place at that time may not have been as significant to the over-extended Muslim empire as it was made out to be by western historians, but it does mark the beginning of a Muslim retreat from the north and the consolidation of Arab power in most of Spain. This consolidation was strengthened by the arrival in 756 of the only remaining member of the Umayyad dynasty, recently replaced by the Abbasids in the central lands of the Muslim world. Abd al-Rahman I and his successors until 976 were the true creators of Muslim Spain. Directly or indirectly they were in control of most of the peninsula except for the extreme north-west; and the old Visigothic capital of Toledo as well as Saragossa on the way to Barcelona became Muslim towns. But their centre was in Andalusia, in Seville, and especially in Cordova, which, together with the new royal city of Madinah al-Zahra, became in the tenth century one of the world's greatest centres of art and culture. It was an Islamic civilization whose models and memories frequently came from the heart of the Muslim world – from Syria, Arabia and Iraq. But, especially in the arts and in social structure, it acquired a uniquely Andalusian flavour. Its artistic forms – the arches of Cordova, the ornamental sculptures from Madinah al-Zahra, or carved ivory caskets and other objects – are easily recognizable as different from com-

7. Plan of the Alhambra:

1. *Vermilion Towers*
2. *Alcazaba*
3. *Gate of Arms*
4. *Gate of Law*
5. *Palace of Charles V*
6. *Puerta del Vino*
7. *Court of the Myrtles*
8. *Tower of the Peinador de la Reina*
9. *Court of the Lions*
10. *Torre de las Damas*
11. *Partal*
12. *Oratory*
13. *Tower of the Captive*
14. *Tower of the Infantas*
15. *Gate of the Seven Heavens*

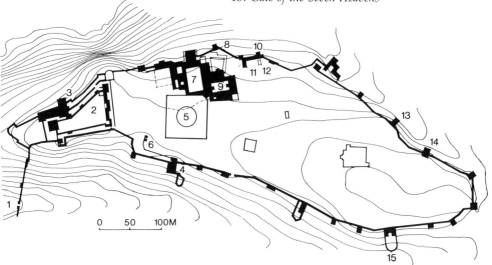

parable forms elsewhere in the Muslim world. And socially it was a culture which succeeded in creating and in many ways maintaining a unique symbiosis between Arab aristocrats, Muslim Arab or Berber soldiers and settlers, a Christian majority in many places except the main cities, and a sizeable and constantly growing Jewish minority.

After the death of al-Hakam II in 976, the political history of Muslim Spain is not a happy one. The Christian Reconquista becomes the dominant force in the peninsula. Slowly, with many vicissitudes and turns of fortune, but inexorably, Spain became Christian. Toledo fell in 1085, Cordova in 1246, Seville in 1248. Muslim reaction took the form of several incursions, initially successful but ultimately failing, of fanatical and puritanical dynasties from Morocco, the Almoravids and the Almohads. There are many reasons for their failure, but one was certainly that Islamic Spain had transformed itself from a reasonably unified entity under the aegis of the caliphs in Cordova into a disunited collection of princelings based on individual cities, the so-called *Reyes de Taifas*, 'the party kings', who fought among themselves more than against the enemy from the north. It is true of course that some of their courts were quite brilliant and that some of the greatest poets, writers, and philosophers of western Islam flourished during these times of political decadence. Ibn Hazm or the great Ibn Rushd (Averroes), not to speak of Maimonides, all belong to these centuries. And, while for the arts these centuries are not particularly brilliant – or rather not well-known, despite the Giralda in Seville or the Aljaferia in Saragossa – they witnessed the first major examples of one of the most characteristic phenomena of Spanish art, the adoption of Muslim themes by Christian and Jewish patrons.

I shall return later to a few aspects of this phenomenon. Its importance at this stage is that it illustrates the impossibility of seeing the Reconquista simply in terms of a Christian takeover of formerly Muslim provinces. In fact a new and immensely complex symbiosis took place, in which political and cultural changes did not entirely coincide. Even political relationships were not clear-cut. Just as in Cordovan times many a Christian prince was the vassal of the Muslim caliphs, so after the strong Christian push of the middle of the thirteenth century, the last Muslim kingdom, the one in Granada, survived by being under theoretical Christian suzerainty. It is one of the paradoxes of the Alhambra that this presumably most Islamic monument was built at a time when Islamic Spain seemed to be hardly Islamic at all. The answer lies partly in the unique development of Granada and of the hills above it.

During the first centuries of Islamic rule Granada was over-shadowed by the town of al-Birah (Elvira), situated a half-day's journey to the west, and Roman and Visigothic remains found in

Granada itself attest to some early settlement there. These pre-Islamic remains, as well as most Islamic ones, are concentrated on the spur known today as the Alcazaba Cadima (*al-Qasbah al-qadimah*, 'the old city'), on the opposite side of the Darro from the Alhambra. Little is known about any constructions from these early centuries; but a mosque, whose traces may have remained in a later building, and an official administrative centre or *dar al-'imarah* typical of all early Muslim settlements were certainly there. The rather small Muslim community does not seem to have spread initially into the flat plain, where Christians and Jews predominated. Whether or not the Alhambra hill was occupied at all is a moot question. A few Roman and Visigothic remains have been found there, but their archaeological context is unclear. Then in the ninth century a governor took refuge during a revolt in a fortress called al-Hamra. Even if this is correctly located at the westernmost point of the Sabikah, it cannot have been much more than a very simple refuge of convenience, for there is no other mention if its existence. In fact hardly any archaeological evidence has been found which can be dated to early Islamic times with any certainty.

The first major change which transformed Granada from a minor provincial town to a city of some importance occurred in the early eleventh century when the Berber dynasty of the Zirids formed a semi-independent principality typical of this confused century in Spanish Islamic history. Under the three rulers Habus, Badis, and Abdallah (1025–90) the city increased in population; and, what is far more important to us, we begin to know something about its buildings. They were concentrated on the Alcazaba hill and its immediate surroundings. The city walls of this time have been partially preserved; a small bath, probably of the eleventh century, survives;[3] and on the Albaicín hill (named from *rabad al-Bayyazin*, 'suburb of the falconers') to the north-west, a palace was built, with a tower provided with an elaborate bronze sculpture of a cock apparently carrying a rider with a shield and a lance.[4] This rather peculiar creation, usually interpreted as a weathervane, was certainly an imitation of the celebrated armed rider on top of al-Mansur's eighth-century palace in Baghdad; the interesting point is that, quite consciously, a theme from the remote imperial capital of early Islamic times was there taken over by a minor Berber dynasty. It is, of course, unfortunate that the building itself has not survived, not even in a later representation,[5] but the connection with Baghdad is important in identifying one of the sources of princely mythology in medieval Andalusia.

For the formation of the Alhambra the most important event is the construction by the Jewish vizier of the Zirids, Yusuf ibn Naghrallah, of a fortress-palace (called *hisn* in the sources) on the Alhambra hill. It is not clear whether this was finished before Yusuf was murdered in 1066, but one account definitely accuses the vizier of building, or wanting to build, a more impressive palace than the king's. In his spirited study of the Alhambra, Bargebuhr has argued that surviving fragments of eleventh-century masonry walls in the Alhambra – of which there are several – can be interpreted as belonging to this palace, and that the celebrated Fountain of the Lions [82 and 83] belonged originally to Yusuf's palace; Bargebuhr points out that an almost direct description of the fountain as it appears now is found in an eleventh-century poem by Ibn Gabirol.[6] The lions appear to be closer in style to eleventh–twelfth-century than to fourteenth-century sculpture, and the present basin was certainly not made originally for them. The lions may, therefore, have belonged to an eleventh-century fountain.[7] And Ibn Gabirol's poem, to which we shall return in detail in the next chapter, would seem to imply that these lions and the fountain to which they belonged were originally in the palace of the Jewish vizier. However, there is not enough archaeological information to draw any wider or further parallel between this eleventh-century palace and the one known today as the Alhambra. And indeed any such parallel would be very unlikely, because several centuries separate them. But, while the Jewish palace of the eleventh century may not have been of major importance for the physical character of the existing Alhambra, its ideological themes, as reflected in poetry, are of extraordinary significance for an explanation of the later Muslim monument, and it is almost certain that it was the first major princely construction attempted on the hill.

There may have been other, purely military constructions on the Sabikah in the Zirid period, but they are difficult to distinguish with precision; altogether, the eleventh century is important for us mainly as the time when the town of Granada came into its own as a significant Muslim city and for the first time a major building was erected on the highest hill overlooking it.

The following century and a half are eventful enough, as Granada was heavily involved in the wars and politics of the Almoravids and Almohads, the two Berber dynasties which sought to stop the reconquest of Andalusia by Christians. It is likely, although the evidence is contradictory, that some of the non-Muslim population left or was evicted and that as a result the proportion of Muslims increased. But these do not seem to have been major centuries for architectural or other artistic achievements, and one can only presume that walls and other fortifications, in part possibly on the Sabikah, were built and repaired.

The year 1238, on the other hand, marks the second turning point in the history of Granada. Muhammad ibn Yusuf ibn Nasr, known as Ibn al-Ahmar, a feudal prince claiming descent from a Companion of the Prophet in Arabia, took the city and, through judicious diplomacy and the acceptance of Castilian suzerainty, managed to maintain himself not merely in Granada but also as the sole ruler of what was left of Muslim Spain. His twenty-two descendants of the Nasrid dynasty ruled until the Christian conquest of 1492. Theirs was on the whole a sad political history, full of intrigues, battles, murder, and treachery. Even the two most successful reigns – Yusuf I (1333–54) and Muhammad V (1354–9 and 1362–91) – were far from peaceful, although they do not match in complexity and tragedy the last fifty years of the dyn-

8. *The Towers of the Captive and of the Infantas*

asty, so vividly described by Chateaubriand and Washington Irving. But the paradox of Nasrid Andalusia lies in the fact that a decadent, indeed moribund political and military power coincided with a strikingly rich and original culture. Its components have recently been described at some length by R. Arié,[8] and three of them deserve particular note here. One is that these were centuries of considerable economic prosperity and wealth; the superbly organized and justly celebrated agriculture of southern Spain was operating at its best, and the traditional Islamic urban bourgeoisie of Muslim and Christian merchants and artisans continued to serve a vast Mediterranean world. The second feature is that, since the area round Granada became a refuge for displaced Muslims from elsewhere, the process of Islamization begun in previous centuries was completed; in a curious way Granada was most Muslim just before the Christian conquest and at a time of partial Christian political suzerainty. Supported by an army largely of African mercenaries, a legalistically rigid Islam in uneasy alliance with a revived mysticism developed there, as though the constricted and threatened Muslim community sought to define most emphatically its unique values. Finally, here, as elsewhere in the late Middle Ages, it was a time of erudite, if not always original, fascination with past literary traditions, generally Islamic and most specifically the brilliant poetry of earlier Andalusia. Learned and elegant, courtly literature is best illustrated by Ibn al-Khatib (1313–74), political leader and brilliant littérateur, and by his protégé Ibn Zamrak (1333–93), whose poetry decorates the Alhambra. And, although the point is of less importance for our purposes, these were centuries of major development for the more popular literature whose impact on romance literature has so often been discussed.[9]

It was, therefore, in a world which was politically unstable, economically prosperous, intellectually constricted and self-centred, poetically rich if not always original, fascinated with the past, and immensely erudite that the Alhambra was created in the form in which we know it. The founder of the Nasrid dynasty may not have lived there himself, but it was he who began to transform the earlier fortress, itself probably embodying the ruins of a Jewish palace, into the huge complex which was eventually to be occupied by Ferdinand and Isabella in 1492.

Unfortunately it is impossible to provide a fully documented chronology of the Alhambra.[10] Too much literary, epigraphic, or archaeological evidence is lacking. Nor is it likely that a complete and fully documented history will ever be written. The Alhambra was not, like Versailles for instance, dominated by the character of its original patron and creator (even though altered occasionally to suit tastes and fulfil new functions). Nor was it, like the Kremlin or the Palatine hill, a succession of formal buildings reflecting various aesthetic, symbolic, and practical needs over several centuries. The Alhambra was in fact a town, a full-fledged city of 740 by 220 metres, surrounded by walls and by gardens to the east and probably to the south. It had all the necessities of a medieval Islamic urban order and probably enjoyed the whole range of a city's social and economic activities, although the fact that it also contained royal residences may have imposed some limits on the development of the former. It was as a city, or at any rate as a full quarter of a city, that it was occupied by the Spaniards, and, in consequence, its archaeology is as confused as that of any living organism. For over five hundred years generations of Muslims and Christians used most of it as a setting for whatever life they chose to live. Muslim princes in the fourteenth and fifteenth centuries, Christian aristocrats and monks in the sixteenth, gypsies and romantics in the nineteenth, tourists and innkeepers in the twentieth have constantly altered whatever they found, not because they were squatters (as in the Roman forum, for instance), but because the Alhambra had been created for continuing living.

In short, from the middle of the thirteenth century onwards the Sabikah hill became a princely city overlooking another, bourgeois, city in the plain below. A few and only a few chronological landmarks in its development can be found in texts

9. *The Tower of the Peinador de la Reina*

and formal inscriptions, and even chronicles provide only minimal information about the life and the events which may have taken place in the buildings. It is, in fact, not very likely that any long and precise descriptions of the palatial establishments or of royal ceremonies were ever written; nor, probably, were systematic recordings ever made of work done. For such sources are very rare in the Muslim tradition; when they do occur, as in Nasir-i Khosro's description of the Fatimid palaces in Cairo, or Bayhaqi's account of the palace of Mas'ud in Afghanistan, they are the result of unusual circumstances, a special permission in the case of the immensely curious Persian traveller, and the personal involvement of Bayhaqi in court affairs.[11] The only partial exception occurs with the palace of Baghdad, whose uniqueness within the Muslim tradition is thus once again emphasized.[12] The questions thus raised for the Muslim palace in general and for the Alhambra in particular are whether the absence of accounts implies that a palace's forms and functions were almost always of a redundant and expected kind which did not warrant description, so that only the exceptional was recorded, or, alternatively, that the palace was outside the mainstream of the culture's awareness of itself and desire to commemorate itself.

We shall return to this fundamental question in conclusion. In the meantime a few reasonably certain chronological points about the Alhambra may be mentioned. In all likelihood the outer enclosure and the aqueduct were completed by the end of the thirteenth century. The gardens and pavilions of the Generalife, higher than the Alhambra, date apparently from the reign of Isma'il (1314–25): but the most important remains in the Alhambra itself – the complexes of the Courts of the Myrtles and of the Lions, the bath which separates them, several of the gates, and the mausoleum near the palace – belong to the times of Yusuf I (1333–54) and Muhammad V (1354–9 and 1362–91). Only one major construction, the interior of the Tower of the Infantas, is as late as the middle of the fifteenth century. But this rough scheme, even though it is now generally accepted, is on the whole based on limited evidence. Only one point is demonstrable on epigraphical as well as architectural grounds. This is that, by the second reign of Muhammad V in the latter part of the fourteenth century, most of what now remains was already there and for the most part in use. In as much as this happens to be when the most brilliant parts of the Alhambra were created, the descriptions which follow attempt to identify what can be presumed to have existed around 1370–1400. Although in a few instances I shall interpret some of the features of the monument, these interpretations are limited to parts that will not be discussed later; my main purpose is to identify the main elements of the Alhambra so as to facilitate the discussion in the following chapters.

WALLS, TOWERS, GATES[13]

The first impression of the Alhambra is of a fortified enclosure, some 2,200 metres in perimeter, whose peculiar shape is obviously determined by the contours and defensive possibilities of the terrain [1–3 and endpaper]. This enclosure was connected, in all likelihood, to the outer walls of the city at two points. At its westernmost end a wall which is still preserved led to the Vermilion Towers and in some unknown fashion connected with the wall surrounding the city from the south. Then at some distance to the north-east of the wall's westernmost edge traces remain of a wall which went down into the valley of the Darro and was probably part of the city's eastern and northern walls. A third connection with city walls is proposed by some authors[14] on the eastern side, but its archaeological or literary justification is not entirely clear. In any event the Alhambra was both a part of the city of Granada and remained independent of it, with its own direct contacts with the outside world.

The impressively thick walls are of hard rubble faced with stone and brick masonry and covered with plaster. There are twenty-two towers, rather irregularly spaced in plan but adapted to the needs and requirements of the terrain. The towers have several notable peculiarities. First, they are not all alike: some are fairly simple and massive square towers [8]; others either project towards the outside, almost like independent units of varying shapes, or they form large or small square units, with many windows and other types of openings [9], and (as we will see later) contain major palatial establishments. The second peculiarity is that the latter group of towers is particularly characteristic of the northern side of the Alhambra, where nature itself provides the best defence. It seems that, whenever military considerations were secondary, towers tended to be transformed into constituent parts of non-defensive units within the enclosure. This immediately raises the question whether the walls and towers are correctly interpreted as defensive or whether they were not simply a formal means of separating the aristocratic and royal area from the other one; the point of these walls and towers may have been less one of protection than of separation. Alternatively, the difference between the northern and south-western towers may be explained by the fact that the two groups correspond to entirely different sections of the interior, the northern being the zone of palaces, the southern being the city. It has been argued that there was a wall between the two zones inside the city itself,[15] but the archaeological evidence, such as it is, does not seem absolutely convincing.

In any event, the walls and towers can be interpreted as simply defensive and protective, as means of separating different kinds of lives, as reflections of internal planning, or as any combination of these purposes. But, whatever complexities one can introduce into their interpretations, a contemporary awareness of their military potential is established by the fact that one could move freely along the northern wall by utilizing passageways under the main palaces and avoiding the main royal complexes. Whether or not these passages pre-date the fourteenth-century constructions above them remains a moot question.

Four main gates (other than posterns or late openings) led into the great Alhambra enclosure. The first and most important one, on the south-western side, is the *Bab al-Shari'ah*, the Gate of Justice or, more precisely, the Gate of Law, dated by an inscription of 1348 [10–12]. It is in several ways unusual. Its peculiar projection and the fact that the formal doorway with the official foundation inscription is perpendicular to the wall may be explained by the sloping terrain on which it was built, but other features are more difficult to interpret. One is the deep porch in front of the entry, as though some ceremony took place there. The ceremonial character of the monument is further emphasized by several architectural and decorative details. For instance the interior with its two turns utilizes three different kinds of vault, an elongated cross vault, a cupola, then three traditional cross vaults; it is almost as though the architect or the patron sought to show off his technical versatility. On the front of the building a hand was carved on the keystone of the arch, while a key with a cord appears on the centre of the inner archway, and the Muslim profession of faith was carved on the handsome capitals of the engaged columns framing the door. The first two of these symbols are not altogether clear, and became a subject of debate as early as in Théophile Gautier's description[16]; and the occurrence of the formal 'There is no God but God, Muhammad is His Prophet, There is no force or power except in God' is rare on gates to fortresses, especially when independent of the dedicatory inscription. Finally, if it is correct to assume that the outer walls of the Alhambra belong to the latter part of the thirteenth century, this gate, with its formal inscription, its unusual name and construction, and its decoration, must have been a fourteenth-century addition of Yusuf I with apparently very specific symbolic and functional purposes.[17] Much has been made of its name, the Gate of Islamic Law, and some have argued that it was the place where justice was meted out. Since this interpretation is connected with the much broader problem of the ceremonial,

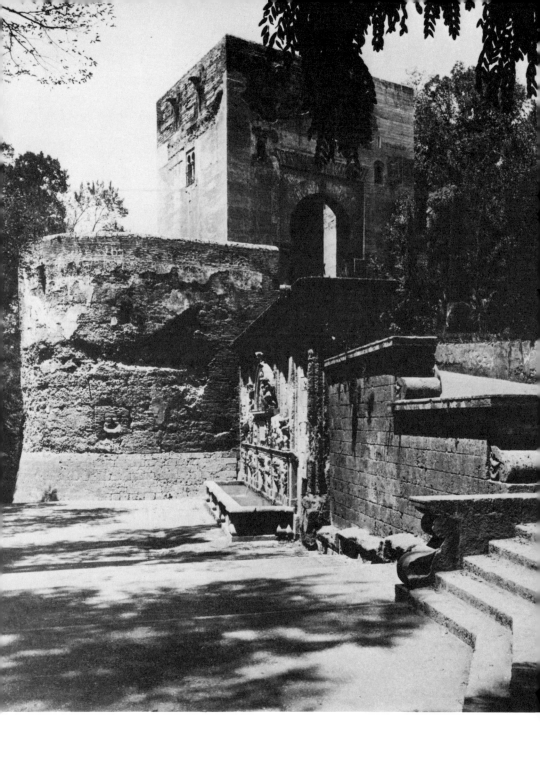

10. *The Gate of Law*

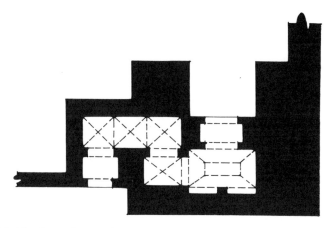

11. *The Gate of Law, plan*

12. *The Gate of Law, inscription*

symbolic, or practical meanings to be given to various parts of the Alhambra, its discussion will be postponed to the next chapter.

The second door on the south side, now known as the Gate of the Seven Heavens,[18] had originally the far more prosaic name *Bab al-Ghudur*, 'Gate of the Cisterns' [13]. With its huge semi-circular projecting bastion and its twenty-two-metre-high

towers, it is the most impressive of the Alhambra gates, even though its forward bastions were blown up by Napoleon's retreating army. But, impressive as it is, it has only a single turn and is in plan quite unexceptional.

The third gate, on the north-eastern side, is the ancient Iron Gate (*Bab al-Hadid*), known today as the Arrabal Gate and connected with the primarily defensive complex of the Torre de los Picos.[19] It was apparently the main way of reaching the Generalife and seems to have been primarily a private passageway rather than a formal entry into a palatial compound. As

with so many other 'Gates of Iron' found all over the Muslim world, it is possible that the original name was *Bab al-Jadid*, 'the New Gate', and that the association with metallic solidity is but a scribal preference over mundane novelty, the letters for 'J' and 'H' being almost identical in Arabic.

The last of the Alhambra gates is the Gate of Arms, almost at the extreme west of the enclosure [14].[20] It was the only gate connecting the Alhambra directly with the city of Granada. Difficult to reach from the outside, it rose into the oldest fortified part of the Alhambra and is justly celebrated for its superb vaults.

THE CITADEL (ALCAZABA)

The westernmost part of the Alhambra is a fortress still known as the Alcazaba (al-Qasbah). Like so many medieval castles, it is a striking monument with one tower – the celebrated Vela on which the flags of Ferdinand and Isabella were set in 1492 – at one end, and three smaller towers at the other, surrounding an irregularly shaped open area, where excavations have brought to light small houses and other buildings difficult to interpret[15]. A *chemin de ronde* goes round the Alcazaba; and its stables, near the Gate of Arms, are still preserved. For the history of fortifications and of vaulting as used in military architecture, the Alcazaba is of considerable interest, especially the Vela Tower with its central core of superimposed cross-vaulted chambers surrounded by barrel-vaulted passageways. It has generally been agreed that much of the Alcazaba dates from before the Nasrids, and it is indeed likely that this is so, although only detailed masonry and stratigraphic studies would establish the exact chronology of the citadel's history. The Alcazaba served as the barracks, the military depot and, in all likelihood, the jail of the Alhambra in the fourteenth century, as it did until very recent times. The whole Alcazaba is strangely devoid of epigraphic information, which may mean either that comparatively few repairs and changes were carried out there during the fourteenth century or that later changes in use and restorations eradicated any inscriptions there may have been.[21]

THE MEXUAR COMPLEX[22]

With what we may, for simplicity's sake, call the Mexuar complex, we penetrate into the most important and best-known part of the Alhambra, the Casa Real Vieja, the Old Royal Residence, or Royal Palace. Instead of dealing with it as a single monument, as it appears on plans [endpaper] and as visitors usually see it, I have divided it into five parts. This division is arbitrary in some details, but it seems justified by the facts that the palace was built

15. *The Alcazaba, interior*

16. *View towards the Court and Gallery of Machuca*

in sections with problematic relationships to each other and that the modifications carried out in them over the centuries are so varied as to preclude a comparable understanding of all the parts, or even a consistently systematic description of them.

The Mexuar complex is in reality a hodge-podge of ruined or restored features at the western end of the palace. A court, 14·60 metres square, which is encountered first, is surrounded by long halls, apparently commons; at the south-eastern corner there is a small mosque, with an adjoining square building which could have been a minaret; there are traces of marble and tile decoration on some of the walls. Then there is a second and larger (22·50 metres) court with a pool in the middle; nothing is clear about its southern side, but to the north there is a portico known as the Gallery of Machuca (the name of Charles V's architect, who lived in the Alhambra and carried out many repairs on it) [16] and a small, much rebuilt tower, with a modern exterior passageway over the outer wall leading to a small oratory with a deeply set mihrab [17]. This second court is higher than the first, and the subsequent one is higher still. It is that which is called the Mexuar, and it consists of a long covered room which, originally, must have been wide open towards the west, almost like a deep portico. A handsomely restored gate with stucco decoration and wooden eaves leads to it from the south and serves today as the entrance into the palace [16, foot]; the interior is curiously divided into a front part with four marble columns supporting a heavy entablature faced with carved stucco under a flat wooden roof and then a gallery [18]. The latter is probably of the sixteenth century, when so much was redone in the room, but both the tile decoration of the lower walls and the partially preserved stucco decoration are of restored Muslim workmanship.

Two key questions are posed by this group of buildings: their date and their function. Since the name of Isma'il (d. 1325) appears on one of the inscriptions in the covered room alongside numerous inscriptions with the titles of Muhammad V, there is no doubt that this is an area that was used throughout the

17. The oratory near the Mexuar, detail of the mihrab

fourteenth century; it is furthermore possible that the lower courts belong to an earlier phase, because their plan is quite different from anything known elsewhere in the Alhambra and because communication between these courts and the rest of the palace is rather clumsy, as though discrete units had been arbitrarily connected. But, while we can be certain that most of these courts and rooms were in use in the fourteenth century, it is impossible to say how much earlier any of them were built.

It is difficult to understand their function, especially that of the Mexuar room itself. The accepted interpretation, developed by Torres Balbás and followed by many scholars, is that the latter was the place of the *Mashwar*, the royal tribunal, while the succession of courts to the west formed a sort of entrance complex

18. The Mexuar, interior

with various service functions. It may or may not be true that in the fourteenth century access to the palace lay through these courts, but neither possibility can be proved.

As to the *Mashwar*, some evidence for a hall reserved for this essentially administrative function exists in a contemporary poem by Ibn Zamrak from around 1365. In addition, Marmol, the great Spanish traveller of the seventeenth century, who left a lengthy account of Granada and of Muslim Africa, described the practice of holding tribunals at the entrance of palaces. But this interpretation, while not impossible, is open to question. There is no proof that this was the formal entrance to the palace, and the fragmentary inscriptions which remain are either Koranic or poetic. The Koranic fragments (XLVIII, 27, and VI, 59) refer to a mosque and to victories, while the poems are glorifications of the prince (almost certainly Muhammad V) and his work. Moreover, while it is true that the fragment by Ibn Zamrak mentions a building with a specific administrative purpose, nothing indicates that this is the one referred to, and nothing in the room itself suggests that it must have been a royal tribunal. It would seem altogether preferable to accept that the functions of all these very different architectural fragments are simply unknown, except for the two small oratories.

THE CUARTO DORADO[23]

To the east of the Mexuar room there is a very small courtyard with a portico to the north leading to a small long room overlooking the valley [19]. This court, including the room, is known today as the Cuarto Dorado or Golden Court, although in many older books it is called the Court of the Mosque. Very much and quite successfully restored, it is one of the most puzzling and most important parts of the Alhambra. This is so in part because in its northern end it has remains from many different periods, ranging from thirteenth-century capitals to sixteenth-century ceilings, and it is not possible to determine whether the earlier elements were reused in later construction or were leftovers from many successive buildings.

But it is important mainly because of its striking southern end [20], a most extraordinary composition of a wall entirely covered with stucco decoration and pierced by two doors and five windows surmounted by a muqarnas frieze and wooden beams and eaves. Leaving aside the decoration of the wall, about which more will be said later (pp. 160–61), the problem is to identify its purpose. It is in fact a monumental gate into the palaces built or rebuilt under Muhammad V. That it was meant as a royal entrance is indicated by its inscription. This includes, first of all, the celebrated Throne verse of the Koran (II, 256), which is one of the most majestic statements of divine power and ends with the

19. *The Cuarto Dorado, looking north*

following words: 'His Throne comprises the heavens and earth; the preserving of them oppresses Him not; He is the All-high, the All-glorious.' Above the Koranic passage, a poem identifies the wall as being a 'gate where [roads] bifurcate and through [which] the East envies the West.' The Koranic citation and the poem are clear on the official and formal meaning of the monument, and we shall return to the implications of this particular iconographic mode in the next chapter. The important point at this stage is that the two doors are of exactly the same size and the same type. But one of them leads directly back into the forecourts, while the other, through a right-angled passageway, suddenly penetrates into the great Court of the Myrtles. The unique feature of this internal entrance-façade is that its crucial bifurcation within the whole system of communications in the Alhambra is invisible to the eye. Even if in the fourteenth century some other architectural or decorative element existed in the courtyard to suggest the correct directions for movement, this façade appears curiously out of place, too large and too formal to be a mere passageway, compositionally unbalanced in relationship to the small court which precedes it, and lacking a visually clear function, even though the inscriptions emphasize its position as a crossroads within the palace's internal organization.

THE COURT OF THE MYRTLES
AND ITS DEPENDENCIES [24]

The Court of the Myrtles or Patio de Comares, as it was already called in the sixteenth century, forms the centre of the first of the two most celebrated parts of the Alhambra. It is a rectangular (36·60 by 23·50 metres) court with a long and narrow (34·70 by 7·15 metres) pool in the centre. The southern end of the court contains a simple portico on six columns and a modern door, probably corresponding to some older passage [21]. Whatever may have been beyond this passage has been obliterated, but excavations carried out under the adjoining palace of Charles V did not bring to light any major remains,[25] and the two floors which are visible on the south wall (one closed, with small windows, the second an open gallery) were probably mere passageways in the wall itself. The eastern and western sides of the court are curiously ill-composed. Each has five doors, which lead either into single, long, narrow, and windowless rooms or into other parts of the palace; no qualitative distinction or distinction of size is made between them.

21. The Court of the Myrtles, south façade

22. *The Court of the Myrtles, north façade*

The northern side of the court [22] is, quite justifiably, the most celebrated. In elevation it consists of an open portico with a small central cupola, a long hall with corner towers, and finally the huge mass of the Comares Tower. Whether seen as a descending composition, from the defensive crenellation of the top of the tower to the frail columns below, or as an ascending one, from the carefully carved arches below to the raw masonry above, it is a highly thought-out architectonic ensemble. In plan it consists of three units. First there is a gallery [23 and 24], with a magnificent

24. *The Court of the Myrtles, wall decoration in the north gallery*

23. *The Court of the Myrtles, north gallery*

25. *The Court of the Myrtles, niche at the end of the north gallery*

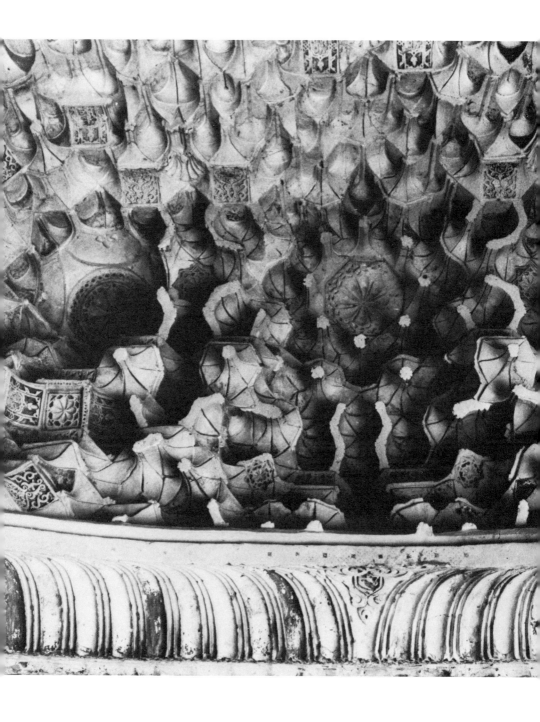

26. The Court of the Myrtles, detail of the same niche

ceiling of wooden marquetry and with highly decorated niches at either end [25 and 26]. Then comes the Sala de la Barca, reached through a handsomely decorated doorway [27]. It is most celebrated for its wooden ceiling, beautifully reconstructed after a fire in 1890 [28]. The Sala de la Barca communicated directly with various other parts of the palace complex to the east and the west, but the nature and purpose of these means of communication are not very clear.

27. *The Court of the Myrtles,*
niche between the north gallery and the Sala de la Barca

28. *The Sala de la Barca, corner detail showing the wooden ceiling*

Finally one penetrates into the so-called Hall of the Ambassadors, a square room (11·30 metres square, and 18·20 metres high), occupying the upper part of the largest and highest (45 metres) external tower of the Alhambra [29 and 30]. In plan it is quite simple: an empty central space with three alcoves, or rather openings pierced through the walls, on all sides other than the entrance and overlooking directly, without apparent barriers, the valley below [31]. What makes the hall so striking are its decoration of tiles and stucco on the walls and its ceiling of 8,017 pieces of different-coloured woods [32 and 33]. We shall have much more to say about this celebrated hall when we discuss both its meaning and its forms, but two points are significant at this preliminary stage. The first is that the tile and stucco decoration of the central alcoves [34 and 35] is richer and more complex than that of the side ones, thus introducing two main axes in an apparently central plan. The second point is that, while it is indeed obvious that this hall was a formal room of some sort, its identification as *the* reception hall of the palace, in which the royal throne would have been placed in the central northern alcove, has been based so far on a single sixteenth-century document, an

29. *The Hall of the Ambassadors, section*

30 and 31. *The Hall of the Ambassadors:*
(below) exterior; (overleaf) interior, looking north

32. *The Hall of the Ambassadors, interior*

account by the royal interpreter Alonso del Castillo. In itself the internal arrangement of the hall does not necessitate its interpretation as a reception hall, even if it does not preclude its occasional use as such. We shall see that the inscriptions in the hall suggest a much more complex explanation.

That the Court of the Myrtles with its appendages forms a single compositional unit is clear from plan and elevation alike.

More complicated is its chronology. The exterior of the tower may be as early as thirteenth-century; the court itself and some of the smaller units seem to be of the time of Yusuf I; but most of the decoration, if not of the architecture, of the Sala de la Barca and the Hall of the Ambassadors belongs to the time of Muhammad V. It is therefore for this period only that we can draw any sort of conclusion about its use and function.

35. The Hall of the Ambassadors, detail of the central northern alcove

THE BATH AND THE DARAXA[26]

The most interesting feature about the heavily restored bath is its location. Even though it communicates with the Courts of the Myrtles and of the Lions and, on a plan, appears to be a sort of link between them, it is in reality at a much lower level and should more properly be associated with the complex of gardens and buildings, known as the Garden of the Daraxa, leading to the Peinador de la Reina overlooking the valley of the Darro. These gardens and apartments were entirely reconstructed in the sixteenth century, and, even though some of their features may

36. The bath, section and plan

have been influenced by earlier constructions, they cannot be used as evidence for the medieval buildings, except in the very general sense that they were probably the living quarters of the palace, possibly the celebrated Harem which has so titillated writers ever since the sixteenth century. Remains of a house were found beyond the present Garden of the Daraxa, and it seems likely that this area of living quarters extended much further to the east.

37. The bath, main hall, Sala de las Camas

The bath itself [36] is of a classical Islamic compact type with a two-storied main hall on four columns [37] followed by a succession of cold and hot rooms. As in all baths, the vaults of the heated rooms are of interesting workmanship but, in the case of the Alhambra, not really unique. The bath can be dated to the time of Yusuf I, with some later decoration. No information exists about the date of the earliest living quarters beyond the bath.

38. *The Court of the Lions, looking east*

THE COURT OF THE LIONS
AND ITS DEPENDENCIES[27]

This most celebrated part of the Alhambra dates from Muhammad V's time. An aerial view [38] indicates far better than a plan that this was a closed composition of long and square or nearly square units around an open space surrounded by a portico, and that a complex hierarchy of parts was involved, not merely in a quasi-two-dimensional façade-like order (as with the northern end of the Court of the Myrtles) but in three-dimensional space as well. The court itself is rather small (28·50 by 15·70 metres), and its surrounding portico with two projecting pavilions articulates the sides of the court in an unusually complicated manner [39–42].

39. The Court of the Lions, looking north-east

We shall return to its details in Chapter 3; the immediate impression is of a court whose components primarily served an aesthetic purpose.

On the western side of the court there is simply a long hall, the Sala de los Mocárabes, with a Renaissance ceiling. The eastern

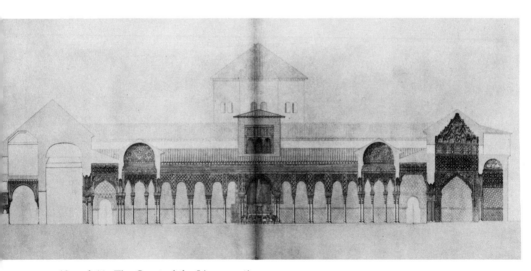

40 and 41. The Court of the Lions, sections

42. *The Court of the Lions, looking west*

end, known as the Hall of the Kings (Sala de los Reyes), is more complex. It consists primarily of three square units, higher than the rest and covered with domes of stucco muqarnas [43 and 44]. These square units are framed and separated by five rectangular spaces with a heavy archway and a flat ceiling [45]. The total effect is of a rhythmic succession of lit and dark parts which seem

43. The Hall of the Kings, ceiling of square unit

44. The Hall of the Kings

45. *The Hall of the Kings*

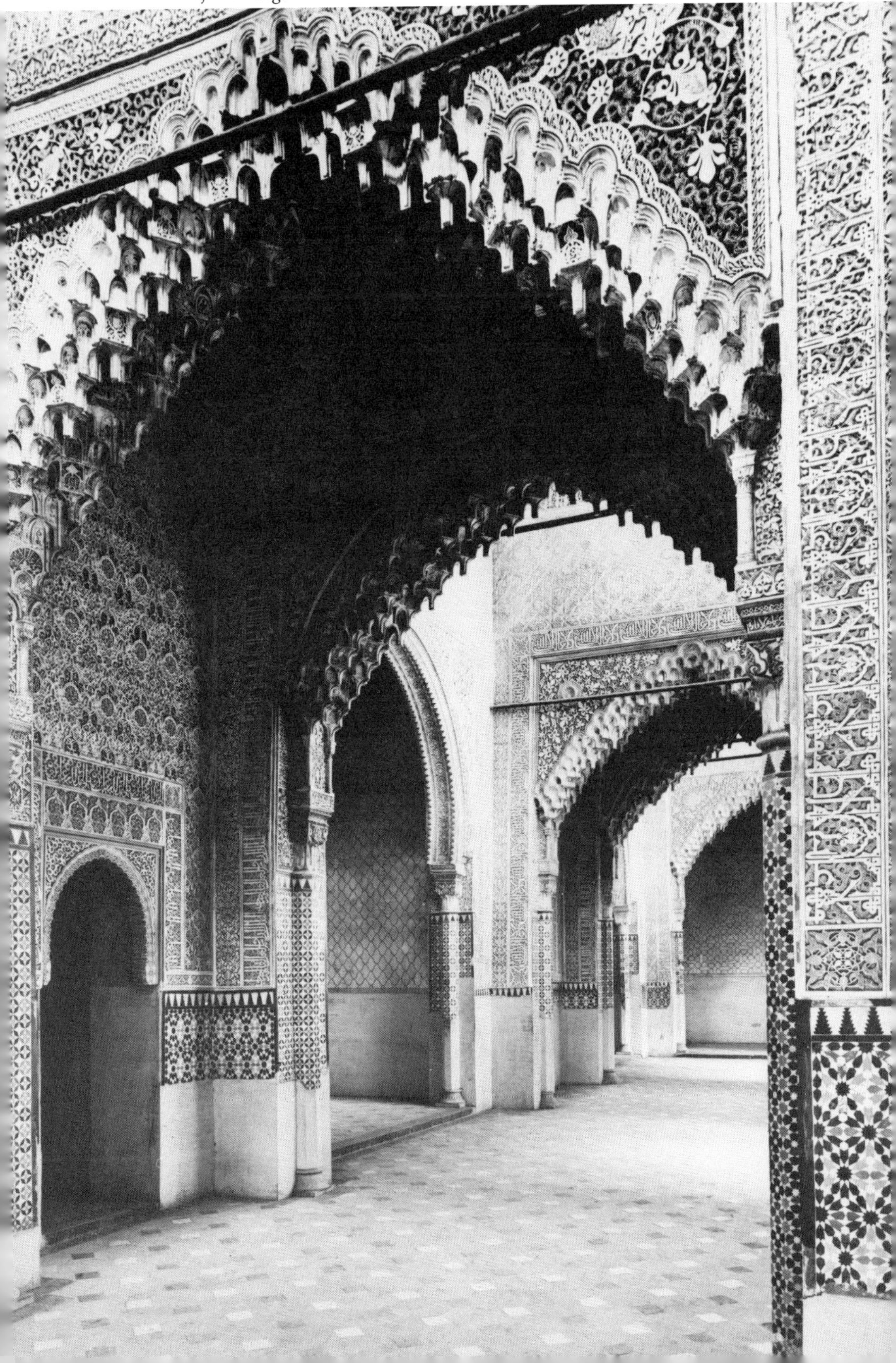

to lengthen the hall. Three alcoves separated by small rooms open from the Hall of the Kings. They are most celebrated for their ceiling paintings [46–8], whose exact iconography and origins have never been worked out but which are probably late fourteenth-century and reflect the impact on the Nasrids of northern, possibly even French taste.[28]

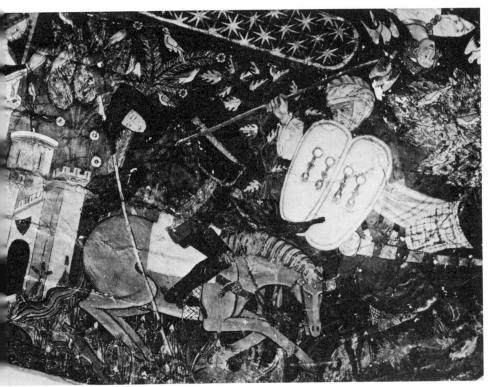

46–8. *The Hall of the Kings, ceiling paintings in the alcoves*

49. *The Hall of the Two Sisters, looking towards the Court of the Lions*

50. The Hall of the Two Sisters, dome

On the north side of the court lies the most impressive part of the complex, the Hall of the Two Sisters [49], so called in romantic memory of two captive sisters said to have perished from love at the sight of the amorous happenings they could witness in the gardens below but in which they could not participate. The hall is a square room with a muqarnas cupola set over an octagon [50]. On three sides it is framed by long rectangular halls. Two of these

51. *The Mirador de la Daraxa*

are merely unlit side rooms, but the northern one leads to a small square pavilion, the Mirador (or lookout) de la Daraxa, which is exquisitely decorated and which overlooks the gardens and apartments below [51]. On the opposite side a much simpler arrangement of a square with two appended rectangular halls is called the Hall of the Abencerrajes [52]. Its cupola is also a muqarnas one but in this instance set over an eight-pointed star [53]. The name derives from that of a family, immortalized by Chateaubriand, whose members were brutally murdered towards the end of Muslim rule in Spain.

52. *The Hall of the Abencerrajes, interior*

53: *The Hall
of the
Abencerrajes,
dome*

There are several inaccessible or unclear features in the south-eastern and south-western parts of the complex and some uncertainty exists about the original means of access into it, although most of it appears to retain its original form. But its purposes and functions are not very clear. The names given to its parts are either descriptive (as with the Lions) or 'romantic', as with the Two Sisters or the Abencerrajes. We shall see that inscriptions (particularly numerous and consisting for the most part of poems written for these buildings) and historical comparisons may provide an explanation, but our initial point must be that a carefully composed and heavily decorated ensemble with halls around a porticoed courtyard does not suggest any other concrete function than sensuous pleasure and excitement for the eyes.

OTHER FEATURES

We can be briefer on other aspects of the Alhambra, either because they have not been as well preserved or because they are less important to its interpretation.

54. *The Partal*

The Partal gardens and the Torre de las Damas[29]

Located on higher ground immediately to the east of the complex of the Lions and the presumed living quarters of the Daraxa, the Partal consists of a large garden, a pool, and a portico with a single tower ending with a mirador overlooking the valley of the Darro [54]. To its side a group of small habitations were discovered with a unique decoration of mural painting: several superimposed friezes of representations of various activities of daily and courtly life, unfortunately very badly preserved. These almost indecipherable paintings are of the late thirteenth or early fourteenth century and therefore pre-date the main buildings to the west. The Partal itself and the charming little oratory set on the walls to the east of it probably belong to the time of Yusuf I.

The Towers of the Captive and of the Infantas[30]

Two towers on the north-eastern side of the Alhambra were transformed into pavilions. One of them, the Tower of the Captive [8], dates from the time of Yusuf I, while the far more

55. The Tower of the Infantas, interior

impressive internal transformation of the Tower of the Infantas [8 and 55] into a series of long halls on several floors around a central shaft belongs to the reign of Sa'ad (1445–61). The latter form the last of the major architectural and decorative efforts in the Muslim Alhambra.

The rawdah[31]

Almost directly to the south of the complex of the Lions, but separated from it by a ditch, stand the poorly preserved ruins of an apparently square building, originally covered with a cupola. In it were found several royal tombstones, and, with the help of a number of texts, Torres Balbás has been able to demonstrate that this building was part of the sepulchral *rawdah* or garden, where at least some of the Nasrid monarchs were buried.

The Puerta del Vino and urban remains

The so-called 'Wine Gate' [56 and 57] stands today outside any archaeological context as one climbs up from the Gate of Law towards the palaces. Its inscription clearly indicates that it was built under Muhammad V, although in its immediate neighbourhood traces were found of earlier walls, and the gate itself looks almost like an addition to an existing wall. It is unique among the

56. *The Puerta del Vino, west side*   57. *The Puerta del Vino, east side*

major gates of the Alhambra in that it was straight and not angled; hence it was probably not defensive at all, as is also suggested by the chamber with a large window above the entrance proper. Seco de Lucena[32] proposed that it was the only remaining door on a wall which, according to his theory, separated the royal enclosure of the Alhambra to the north from the urban development on the southern half of the hill. And it is indeed true that a bath, a mosque, and private houses were identified in the southern part of the enclosure, although none of these are now visible. The hypothesis is possible, but the evidence for a dividing wall seems very slim.

Too little is certain about the physical nature and extent of the urban development inside the Alhambra walls to allow for any sort of definite conclusion, although it seems self-evident that whatever there was must have been concentrated in the southern part of the walled area. From the evidence of the houses near the Partal it may be proposed that the earlier city occupied a larger area and that it was during the reigns of Yusuf I and especially of Muhammad V that the royal palaces became more prominent than the urban centre. The mosque, which has now disappeared, appears to have been built or rebuilt around 1308, and baths as well as whatever is known of houses are also usually dated earlier than the beginning of Yusuf I's main building programme.[33] But all this is very speculative.

THE GENERALIFE[34]

It is difficult to discuss the Alhambra without some mention of the Generalife and the various pavilions and gardens above it. The name itself, known already in the fourteenth century, is a corruption of *Jinnah al-'Arif*, for which two interpretations have been proposed: 'the Garden of the Architect' or 'the Noblest of Gardens'.

Most of the present layout of the gardens themselves is modern, and many of the buildings have been much restored and

58. The Generalife, pool and south pavilion

rebuilt. The importance of the Generalife for our purpose – to set
the archaeological stage for an explanation of the Alhambra – lies
in two of its features. The first, already mentioned, is that some of
it is earlier than the main palaces of the Alhambra, having been
already partly completed by 1319. It may therefore have played a
role in the formation of the palaces, although it is difficult to know

whether this role was accidental, in the sense that its water supplies preceded those of the Alhambra, or whether the Alhambra should be considered as the royal residence built next to already existing princely gardens. The other pertinent feature of the Generalife is that it is typologically a unique combination of a monument which was both public and private, with two independent entrances, one from the Alhambra below, the other from the south and the outside; it seems, therefore, to belong to a somewhat different order of use from the Alhambra proper, less secluded and less restricted. The main part of the Generalife consists of a long pool surrounded by plants [58], with two

59. The Generalife, north pavilion   *60. The Generalife, staircase*

loggias on the long sides and two complexes of buildings at the narrow ends. One was complicated, containing several rooms and interior courts; the other [59] consisted of a portico, a long hall, and a square mirador higher up. Above this main part were more gardens and waterways, including the celebrated one with water running in the handrail of a staircase ramp [60]. These stairs led to an oratory and, even higher up, to several additional pavilions, now mostly gone, one of which had the romantic name of the House of the Bride, *dar al-'Arusah*.

For an elaboration of the history, the aesthetic, and the symbolism of late medieval Granada and of the Alhambra, the importance of the Generalife is considerable. Recent investigations by Bermúdez Pareja and James Dickie have also shown its significance for the history of gardens; but too much has been restored and redone for it to be as important as the Alhambra below in the history of medieval palaces.

The first conclusion which emerges from our brief description of the elements which make up the Alhambra is that a very great deal about this extraordinary monument is unknown, or at least unpublished. This is particularly true of what may be called the anatomy of the monument, its masonry, its foundations, the joints between its walls, the accidental or controlled finds made during excavations. But it is also true of the whole southern half of the walled area, where a mosque, baths and houses once stood. For a full understanding of the Alhambra, the character of this presumed urban area is essential, but we shall probably never know what it was. A precise archaeological description of the whole monument is urgently needed. When detailed information is available – as in the case of the construction of the wooden cupola of the Hall of the Ambassadors – its absence elsewhere only becomes the more regrettable. Identifications of functions and purposes have often been too hastily made by writers relying on passing references or preconceived ideas of a Muslim palace and 'oriental' palace life. The one contemporary document which exists, the inscriptions found almost throughout the Alhambra, has only very rarely been utilized, and it is interesting to note that the most thoughtful pages written on the Alhambra, those of Georges Marçais in his general book on western Islamic architecture, are so full of uncertainties about the history and meaning of the building.[35]

But a number of positive conclusions do emerge, and they lead to the questions we shall seek to investigate. One of these conclusions is that the Alhambra was a miniature city, dominated by a royal establishment. And, so far as we know, this establishment and especially its two main complexes were the last major monuments in the development of the hill. The intriguing question is whether this came about accidentally either because, quite simply, the decline of the Nasrid dynasty after the death of Muhammad V preserved so much of his work at the Alhambra, or because there had been from the very beginning some more or less coherent idea about a palatial establishment which took many decades to reach completion, assuming that it was in fact completed by Muhammad V. Or, to put it another way, the question is how to interpret a monument which was so clearly additive in time, even if its last major patron left traces of his activities almost everywhere in it.

The Alhambra is also a monument which is additive in space: except for certain problematical areas around the so-called Mexuar, each one of the units we have described is a separate entity of its own which could be seen and examined independently. The problem becomes more complex when we recall that, except for a bath, the oratories, and the peculiar gate of the Cuarto Dorado, it is almost impossible to assign precise functions to individual parts of the ensemble. From the architectural and decorative forms alone, no clear image emerges of the activities they housed, and this is especially so in the more impressive units.

Finally it is easy to see that the compositional vocabulary and the constructional or decorative techniques of the Alhambra are relatively limited: towers, courts, galleries, long and square halls, columns, muqarnas domes, wooden ceilings, stucco and tile covering. The question is whether these elements are used throughout in the same fashion or whether there are qualitative or functional variations in them. At first glance there is a repetitive character to most of the Alhambra's elements; but is this impression justified? Is there not some more profound aesthetic and sensuous aspect to its more elaborate parts than that of qualitative superiority? And, if it is merely quality of execution and size which distinguish the Hall of the Two Sisters [49] from the Hall of the Kings [43–5], can one define this quality?

These are the questions to which we shall seek answers. Regardless of what those answers may be, one last conclusion is perhaps less debatable and does not lead to further queries. It was best expressed by the poet of the Alhambra, Ibn Zamrak, who wrote that 'the Sabikah is a crown on Granada's forehead. . .and the Alhambra (may God watch over it) is the ruby on top of that crown.' And in another poem he said that 'Granada is a bride whose crown is the Sabikah, whose jewels and clothes are flowers, . . .whose throne is the Generalife, whose mirror is the surface of its pools, whose earrings are drops of frost.'[36] And it is indeed true that, for reasons as yet unknown, in the thirteenth and fourteenth centuries the whole city of Granada was transformed by this extraordinary backdrop of gardens and palaces between the snow-covered and uninhabited mountains and the surrounding bustling and fertile valley.

Chapter 2

FUNCTIONS AND MEANINGS: THE ICONOGRAPHY OF THE MUSLIM PALACE TRADITION

Although the Alhambra consists of a series of independent units built at different times and without any evident overall compositional scheme, it is possible to identify within it a number of general themes and characteristics which occur with some consistency and through which the building itself, its meaning, and its background can be defined. Some of these themes and characteristics are primarily formal; that is, they are visual impressions and elements of architectural or decorative composition. Appreciation of them leads into rather complex questions of aesthetic judgement, which will be discussed in the next chapter. But the forms themselves are easier to understand if their functions and the symbolic or practical meanings which can be associated with them have been investigated. For Renaissance and post-Renaissance monuments in the West, drawings, projects, contemporary accounts, at times even statements by architects and patrons, exist to help explain how the monument came into being. No such documents exist for the Alhambra, and the chronicles in particular are quite silent on what must have been a major social and economic effort. For the Muslim Middle Ages this silence is not unusual, and we have already pointed out how this lack of documentation complicates any immediate identification of purpose for the components of a Muslim palace. *A priori* we are compelled to assume that the Alhambra's impact was limited to its own internal circle, which did not record in official literature the nature and scope of its aims in developing the palace. It is by comparison with other known monuments and by the internal analysis of its own features that the building must be understood.

To this general observation there is an important exception: the inscriptions found all over the walls of the Alhambra. Since these inscriptions will play a very important part in our discussion, a few words about them are necessary. One must recall that in Islamic art inscriptions replaced the figurative imagery used in other architectural traditions; whatever ornamental role they may have, inscriptions are – or at least can be – indicative of the purposes of a building or the kinds of meanings which were at one time attributed to it.[1] In the Alhambra as in most later medieval Muslim buildings, they are of three kinds, and a complete inscription may contain elements of all three types. One consists of *informative* inscriptions, giving very concrete information such as the time of the monument's construction or the personage by and for whom it was built – as is found, for instance, on the Gate of Law and the Puerta del Vino. A second type may be called *redundant* inscriptions; they use formulas which are consistently repeated and to which, at least at first glance, no particular significance can be given. Indeed, they are often simply dismissed as 'Koranic formulas' or 'pious expressions'. Such are the cartouches found all over the Alhambra repeating endlessly 'Power to our Lord Abu Abdallah' and 'There is no Victorious One except God'. But we shall see that even in this case the redundant formulas are not entirely accidental: it can be argued that the choice of formulas indicates quite consciously the mood a monument sought to convey.

Finally there are inscriptions which can be called *iconographic*, for they can be shown to have been chosen in order to emphasize some special purpose of the building or to make an association which is not *a priori* obvious. The most common source for these iconographic inscriptions is the Koran; and in several instances in the Alhambra, an interpretation of the monument can be proposed through an analysis of its Koranic quotations. But in the

Alhambra a second type of iconographic inscriptions consists of poetry. The use of poetical inscriptions on architecture is not unique to the Alhambra, but, to my knowledge, it is exceedingly rare before the fourteenth century and especially in the Mediterranean world. The earliest instance of poetical inscriptions on architecture discovered so far is found at the other end of the Muslim world, in Ghazni in Afghanistan; it is possibly not an accident that it occurs in a palace,[2] in this instance of the early twelfth century. Poetical motifs became fairly common on Iranian artefacts at about the same time;[3] but other than the Alhambra no example of this use of poetry, either on artefacts or on buildings, is known in the Muslim world west of the Euphrates until quite late in pre-modern times.[4] It is likely, however, that the use of poetry in palaces antedates its common occurrence in Syrian houses of the eighteenth century, for the latter were probably inspired by earlier models. Unfortunately our knowledge of princely dwellings after the tenth century is much too fragmentary to prove the point.

In the Alhambra almost all the rooms, especially the most important ones like the halls around the two main courts and the Generalife, as well as the Fountain of the Lions, are provided with poems. Two features should be mentioned. Most of these poems are at eye level (for instance around the small niches between the Sala de la Barca and the Hall of the Ambassadors, in the axial alcove in the Hall of the Ambassadors [31], in the Mirador de la Daraxa [61] and the Hall of the Two Sisters [49]). Their most common location is just above the tile decoration found on the lower part of most walls. Visitors and others were evidently expected to see and read them. Furthermore the majority of the poetical inscriptions were especially composed for the palace, whether they are all by Ibn Zamrak, the last of the great poets of Muslim Spain, or whether, as has been argued recently,[5] some of them are the work of Ibn Jayyab, who died in 1348. What is important is that the poems are for the most part topical, referring directly not only to the building in general, but to the

61. *The Mirador de la Daraxa, showing poetical inscriptions*

specific parts of the building in which they occur. Often they are put in such a form as to imply that the building itself is speaking and explaining its purpose. Whether original or commonplace in its imagery, it is poetry which was undoubtedly intended to carry an iconographic meaning.

The rarity of comparable examples of poetical inscriptions makes it difficult to relate the symbolism and life they evoke for the Alhambra to what is otherwise known of medieval palaces. Therefore, before examining the poetry in detail, we must try to situate some of the architectural and compositional characteristics of the Alhambra within what is known of the Muslim palace tradition. My choice of themes for this discussion – defence, water, and the faith of Islam – may seem slightly arbitrary, but in fact these are particularly notable themes, selected because they provide the best introduction to the symbolic and ceremonial meanings suggested by the inscriptions.

THE ALHAMBRA AS A FORTRESS

Both its location on top of a hill and many of its features such as walls, gates, and towers lend the Alhambra the appearance of a fortress. But, as was indicated earlier, this fortified and defensive appearance is in part misleading. Some of the towers, for instance the Tower of the Infantas [8], were provided with strikingly unmilitary internal arrangements of lavishly decorated pleasure rooms [55], and the walls are as much a means to separate one world from the other as a formal means of defence, although obviously enough the two functions are not always clearly distinguished. It is even possible that, as the Alhambra developed, a change occurred in the significance of its outer walls and towers. For, if the archaeological history of the monument is correct, the exclusively military Alcazaba and the outer walls were erected before the main palaces, and we have no evidence that the elaborate constructions of Yusuf I and especially of Muhammad V were intended from the beginning, even though

62. Late Roman mosaic from Carthage

the possibility cannot be entirely excluded. What began in the
thirteenth century as a primarily defensive establishment, fully in
accord with the unsettled and embattled world of the time, may
simply have developed into a formal monument in the more
secure fourteenth century. But in the absence of literary and
archaeological evidence all this is hypothetical, and one serious
argument against it is the peculiarity, mentioned earlier, that the
unusually large towers on the northern side, the very ones which
became incorporated into the palace, were from the beginning
planned on a grander scale and with a less obviously defensive
purpose.

Whatever the solution to this primarily archaeological problem may be, the fortified aspect of the Alhambra belongs to two traditions of palace architecture. One seems to have arisen in the Mediterranean in late antiquity and is known in Central Asia as early as in the second century A.D. It is the aristocratic tradition of a private residence set (in most cases) in the country, in all likelihood in the midst of agricultural estates.[6] Such are the late Roman villas depicted on Tunisian mosaics [62], or Khorezmian and Soghdian establishments at the frontier of Central Asia [63].

63. *Merv, Qyz-qalah, probably eighth-century*

Not surprisingly, these examples are in frontier areas and their fortified aspect is easy to explain by politically and socially unsettled circumstances. With the appearance of emperors who began as soldiers, and in a broader sense with the militarization of taste from the late second century onwards, this kind of feudal frontier establishment came to be used in areas of greater security and acquired other meanings and functions than defensive ones; it became an architectural type. The most celebrated examples are the early Islamic châteaux of Syria and Palestine [64], continued on a grander scale in eleventh- and twelfth-century establishments in North Africa [65]. The most illustrious imperial

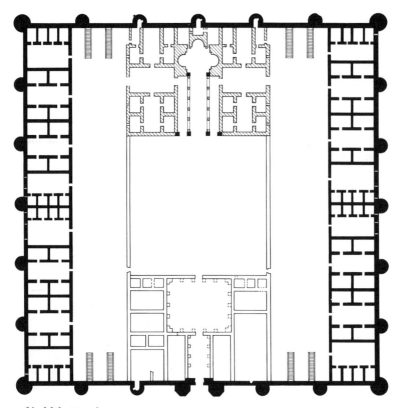

64. Mshatta, plan

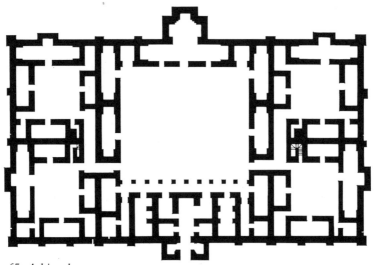

65. Ashir, plan

instance and perhaps the earliest one in the Mediterranean area seems to have been Diocletian's palace at Spalato [66].[7] In almost all these instances the interior aspect of the palace was that of a fort with heavy towers and other defensive features. At times

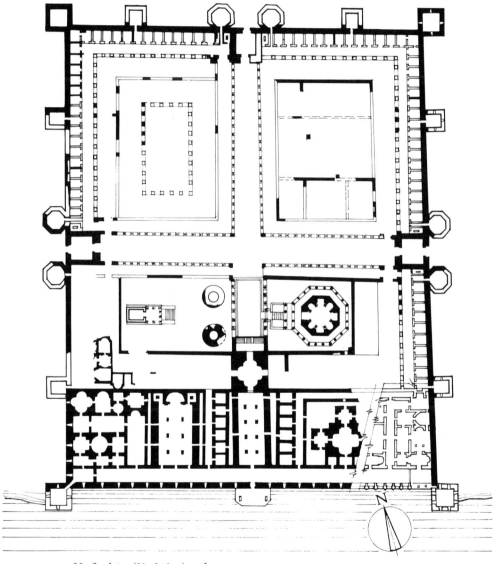

66. Spalato, Diocletian's palace

these military devices were not for actual use, but mere signs of power and authority. The degree of luxury found inside these establishments varied considerably, but as a group they clearly demonstrate the formal association between the prince's prestige and a fortress-like palace in late antique art in the eastern Mediterranean and in the Near East.

The second tradition has a far more ancient and more complicated history. Visible as early as in Sargon II's palace at Khorsabad [67],[8] it is the tradition of a royal city within a larger urban centre. It acquired a variety of forms, which deserve fuller investigation; their pecularities can only be sketched here. In Rome, Byzantine Constantinople, Ottoman Istanbul, and Abbasid Samarra, there were walls separating the royal or imperial compound from the rest of the city, but there is comparatively little evidence that fortifications or military elements (other than at times a formal gate) played a major part either in the practical

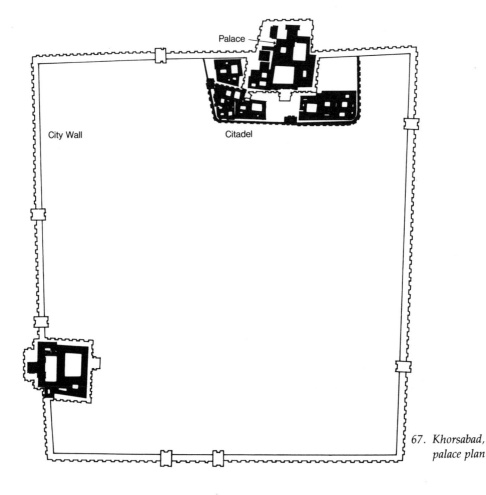

Palace

City Wall

Citadel

67. Khorsabad, palace plan

operation of the palace or in its symbolism. The wall was simply a barrier isolating the royal world from that of common mortals; occasionally, as in Abbasid times,[9] this isolation acquired mythical characteristics, illustrated, among other ways, by the legends attached to the personage of Harun al-Rashid; but on the whole the formal elements identifying the palace were non-military.

A very different form of a city within a city developed with the growth of the citadel, the *qal'ah* of Arabic texts or the *ark* of Persian literature. As early as in the tenth century a passage in the description of the world by Ibn Hawqal dealing with Bukhara[10] describes a citadel which is outside the town but adjoining it. The practice of citadels being part of an urban order but at the same time having independent means of access to the outside world may be explained by the frequency with which rulers and subjects were of different ethnic stock or sectarian allegiance. It is certainly characteristic of the citadels of Aleppo [68 and 69] and

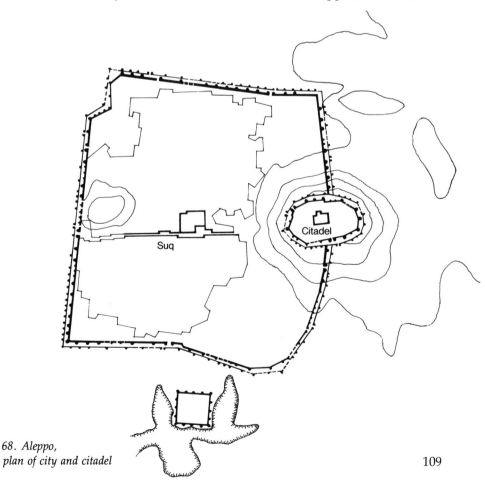

68. Aleppo,
plan of city and citadel

69. *Aleppo, citadel*

Jerusalem[11] or of the whole Fatimid city of Cairo[12] as well as of the
Alhambra. But then Ibn Hawqal adds that the citadel was equal to
a small town in size and contained the castle of princes or gov-
ernors, a major mosque near the gate from the citadel into the
city, a prison, and presumably a number of other buildings for
living and whatever other purposes may have been needed in
tenth-century Bukhara. It was more than a princely and military
compound: it was a miniature city; and Fatimid Cairo was hardly
a mini-town, even though the main area of population was outside its walls.

So far as is known, it was in the tenth century that such separate
princely cities began in the Muslim world, and, again within the
limitations of our present knowledge, it seems that it was on the
Central Asian frontier of Islam that they first appeared. Although
it is not yet possible to demonstrate that the Central Asian practice spread elsewhere, it is curious that from the tenth century

onwards, the large citadel attached in a variety of ways to existing and usually recently walled cities became a fixture of most major urban centres. In Aleppo, the citadel contained a cemetery, some fifty houses or apartments with such names as the House of Power, the House of the Columns, the House of Royalty, baths, and even a hippodrome or a place for military exercises.[13] The Cairo citadel is less precisely known but the presence in it of mosques and elaborate and handsome buildings (for example, the Qasr al-Ablaq of the early fourteenth century, still visible in part in nineteenth-century prints [70], and a House of Justice described by Maqrizi, the great historian of Cairo, in which the sultan held court) indicates that it too formed a whole world independent from and parallel to the bourgeois and popular

70. *Cairo, Qasr al-Ablaq*

world of the city.[14] To a somewhat smaller degree the same development can be demonstrated for Damascus, Jerusalem, Mardin, Diyarbakr-Amida, and any number of other cities.

It is still very much a moot question whether the late antique and early medieval tradition of fortified appearance as an almost compulsory attribute of power carried its formal associations and symbols into the more practical tradition of feudal citadels inside cities. But it does seem clear from the examples of Cairo, Aleppo, Bukhara, and the huge and still imperfectly known eleventh–twelfth-century site of Lashkari Bazar in Afghanistan [71][15] that an independent princely life of occasionally high luxury was lived in fortified citadels.

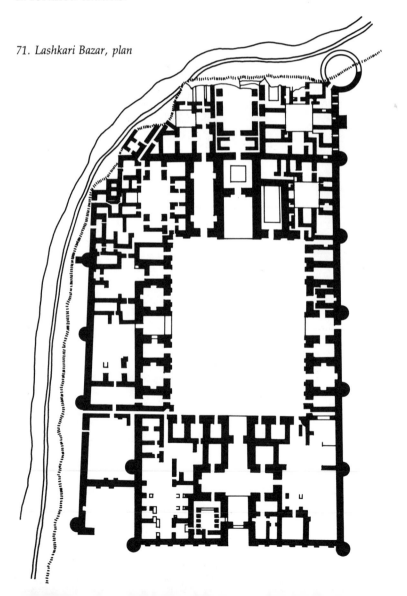

71. *Lashkari Bazar, plan*

The Alhambra is certainly fully in the tradition of these city-citadels, and, if there is anything that it took up from the other tradition of single palaces, it is the peculiarity that some of its towers may have been planned from the beginning for internal development rather than for defensive purposes, just as the mighty towers of Umayyad palaces in Mshatta or Qasr al-Hayr West [72] were useless for any military purpose. As a result the walls actually separate ways of life from each other rather than defend one social or political order against the other. In this fashion the Alhambra summarizes both medieval versions of the fortified princely monument. It is a place whence physical force and control came: popular riots in the lower city were stopped by

72. Qasr al-Hayr West, façade

the Berber guard from the Alhambra, while struggles in the Alhambra itself tended to be limited to aristocratic families. Like Khorsabad two thousand years earlier or contemporary Aleppo, the Alhambra lies astride the walls of the city, being both part of the city and alien to it. It was also the seat of symbolic power; we shall have more to say about this later, but one aspect of this power is already evident: it provided a setting for a different kind of life, the life of princes, as did the palaces of Rome or of Constantinople and Baghdad. Finally it was probably a place of refuge in times of distress, although information is lacking on this score. It differs from Aleppo and Cairo only in its size and in the unusual artistic quality of what remains; perhaps only the Kremlin in Moscow, which is typologically quite close to the Alhambra, has preserved a similar number of unique monuments.

But, while the fortified aspect of the Alhambra is not unusual, one attribute of fortifications which was carried through every unit of the palace and its overall composition is, so far as I know, unique. This is the emphasis on parts separated from each other in such a way that the passage from one to the other is never obvious. In the Alhambra there are no portals or vistas leading from one unit to the other. The Cuarto Dorado [19 and 20] is a gate, but it is also a trap, for it does not indicate the correct direction to take. In fact, the whole palace is like the City of Brass of *The Thousand and One Nights*, where secret passageways and small doors lead the visitor, accidentally and secretly, from one marvellous architectural setting to the next. But, although the result has nothing to do with military or defensive enterprises, the conception was, in origin, very much a military one. And, at the risk of stretching a point, one might argue that even in the internal structure of the Alhambra much is a sort of conscious camouflage. This is perhaps best seen if one looks either at sections of the building [29, 40 and 41] or at the external frame of the complexes of the Lions or the Myrtles [38]. Their visible shells hardly suggest the brilliance or even the actual forms of the interiors. In creating this contrast between exterior appearance

and internal arrangement, the architects of the Alhambra illustrated in a uniquely preserved fashion the deeper meaning of a
palace-citadel or a palace-fort, that it possesses a secret which
construction seeks to defend. The problem lies in the nature of
the secret.

THE ALHAMBRA AND WATER

It was the construction of aqueducts to the Sabikah hill that made
it possible for the Alhambra to develop. The practical advantages
of running water instead of cisterns for daily life are obvious
enough, but two more formal uses of water, the bath and gardens, whose praises were already proclaimed in the fourteenth
century,[16] are far more important for an understanding of the
Alhambra.

The presence of a bath in a Muslim palatial setting is not in the
least unusual. Almost all Umayyad country estates were provided with baths, sometimes very luxurious ones, as at Khirbat
al-Mafjar [73], where an original architectural setting was provided for a stunning display of decorative techniques and

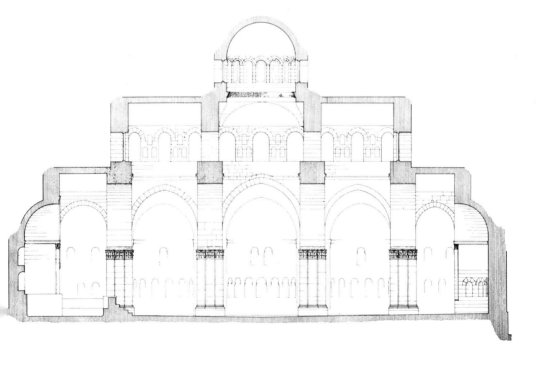

73. Khirbat al-Mafjar, bath reconstruction

motifs.[17] Archaeological evidence of baths in palaces after the eighth century is limited, but literary documents and occasionally architectural fragments prove their continuous existence. Baths were also an urban commodity; thousands are listed in descriptions of cities, and any number have been preserved from the twelfth century onwards.[18] The Alhambra bath is in no way unusual, either in plan or in technique. With its fancily decorated meeting and undressing hall followed by a passageway leading into cold and hot rooms, it belongs to a standard type available in a close enough form in Granada's earlier and much more modest *bañuelo* [74].

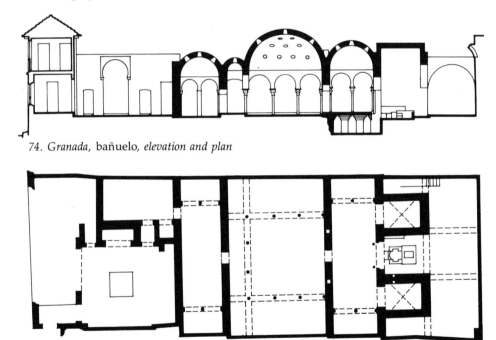

74. *Granada,* bañuelo, *elevation and plan*

There are, however, in the Alhambra bath, several features which, though they may not be very significant in themselves, are indicative of a number of concerns which occur all over the palace. One is that the bath is in a curiously ambivalent rela-

116

tionship to the formal parts of the rest of the monument. It can be reached directly only through the presumed living quarters in the lower patio of the Daraxa and has no immediate access to the two complexes of the Myrtles and the Lions. Yet it is not totally isolated from them. The connection occurs through the windows of the second floor of the bath's main hall [36], and it required the construction of an elaborate tower-like cupola over the hall. Practically invisible and insignificant from the courts, these windows can be used to look into the courts from the bath. Private though its activities may be, the bath becomes a place from which the official or semi-official events of the palace can be witnessed. A related theme of formal meaning in highly private setting derives from an inscription which was originally near two lion-heads used as spouts.[19] It compares hot water to the protective force of the prince and cool water to his generosity. And it ends with the following two verses: 'Thus how many wonderful things brighten up the one who marvels at this noble place! Is there anyone like Abu al-Hajjaj [Yusuf I], our sultan, who does not desist from triumph and great victory.' Read in isolation these verses are no more than poetic hyperbole or clichés, but in as much as their sentiments appear in many other parts of the palace, they suggest metaphorically that even so prosaic an activity as bathing and the well-being it provides are gifts and symbols of an ever-victorious prince.

Gardens, pools, and fountains, of course, represent much more original and much more important uses of water. They have also been studied and described more fully and more frequently, although only rarely in connection with the architecture of the building itself and without leading to hypotheses about their meaning. The association of water with gardens occurs in the Alhambra in two main ways. One, as in the Court of the Myrtles, the Partal and the Generalife, is essentially static in the sense that either a single long pool or two, as in the Generalife, appear as the main axes of compositions, and trees, shrubs, or flowers are planted around them. The other, as in the Court of the Lions, is a

75. *Khirbat al-Mafjar, pool, section*

dynamic one, whereby two water-axes rise in adjacent rooms and then move towards the centre of the court to be returned to the fountain and spilled through the lions' maws.[20] At this general level, neither is particularly original, for since pre-Islamic times in Iran[21] or in the Mediterranean,[22] through Umayyad or Abbasid examples like Khirbat al-Mafjar [75 and 76], Qusayr Amrah's paintings or Samarra, and all the way to late Iranian and Mughal instances, pools and fountains with or without gardens characterized all palaces and, in smaller form, most houses.[23] Closer to

76. *Khirbat al-Mafjar, mosaic decoration in the bath*

the Alhambra in time and space, Muslim or Norman pavilions in Sicily such as the Zíza in Palermo, the court of the mosque in Seville, or the more spectacular huge pool of the Qal'ah of the Beni Hammad in Algeria [77][24] all exhibited the same features. In

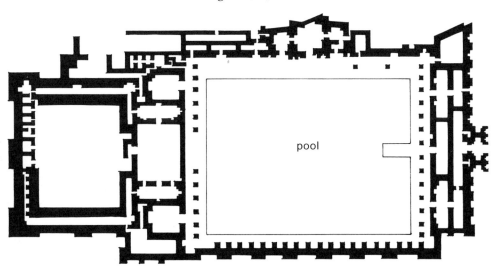

77. *The Qal'ah of the Beni Hammad, plan*

addition, many texts from Spain or Morocco have maintained for centuries the memory of palatial pavilions known as 'houses of water' (in twelfth-century Marrakesh), or huge gardens with elaborate canals and fancy belvederes in the midst of vegetation (in tenth-century Cordova). The most celebrated of these establishments was the imperial palace in Madinah al-Zahra, where a beautiful pavilion on marble columns overlooked a succession of gardens and pools; it even contained a basin with twelve statues of animals, made, as the sources repeat with pride, in Cordova.[25]

There is also little doubt about the most common meanings associated with water and its surrounding gardens. They represented paradise, at times a specifically Islamic holy paradise, as in the use of the word *rawdah* ('garden') for certain cemeteries and burial grounds in the Alhambra as well as in many other places as far east as Afghanistan,[26] at other times a more sensuous paradise of physical well-being whose possible mystical associations should not overshadow occasional orgiastic connotations. The theme of the garden with pools or fountains, with a division of cultivated space into four parts, and with frequently (as has recently been demonstrated for the Generalife[27]) a pavilion in the centre, is easily found in Muslim tradition, as in mosaic representations of the mosque of Damascus [78] and of the Aqsa mosque in Jerusalem [79],[28] in the description of the fourteenth-

78. *Damascus, mosque, mosaic*　　　　　79. *Jerusalem, Aqsa mosque, mosaic*

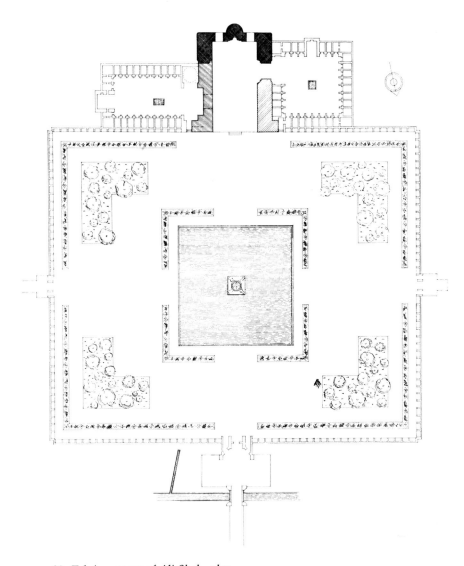

80. Tabriz, mosque of Ali Shah, plan

century Mongol constructions in Tabriz, as well as in the great mosque of Ali Shah, also in Tabriz [80],[29] and in quadripartite gardens or *chehar baghs* of later Iran [81].[30] It is also a theme of Christian thought and imagery, as in the complex iconography and symbolism surrounding the Fountain of Life.[31]

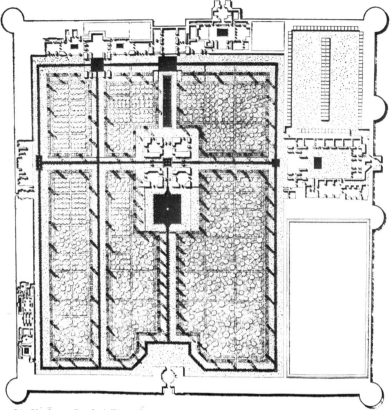

81. Kashan, Bagh-i-Fin, plan

It would thus be fairly easy to conclude that the use of water in the Alhambra simply belonged to a long and well-established tradition of paradisial gardens in palace settings. The main direction for further investigation would be of the sort initiated by James Dickie: to establish as precisely as possible the types of plant arrangements of the Middle Ages (the nineteenth-century arrangements found today being obviously incorrect). However, for the Alhambra two documents exist which make it possible to penetrate deeper in our understanding both of gardens and of water.

The first document is a poem by the fourteenth-century poet of Granada Ibn Luyun. As suggested by Lévi-Provençal[32] and rede-

122

fined by Dickie,[33] the poem belongs to a tradition going back to the Cordovan world of the tenth century.

With regard to houses set amidst garden an elevated site is to be recommended, both for reasons of vigilance and of layout;

and let them have a southern aspect, with the entrance at one side, and on an upper level the cistern and well,

or instead of a well have a watercourse where the water runs underneath the shade.

And if the house have two doors, greater will be the security it enjoys and easier the rest of its occupant.

Then next to the reservoir plant shrubs whose leaves do not fall and which [therefore] rejoice the sight;

and, somewhat further off, arrange flowers of different kinds, and, further off still, evergreen trees,

and around the perimeter climbing vines, and in the centre of the whole enclosure a sufficiency of vines;

and under climbing vines let there be paths which surround the garden to serve as margin.

And amongst the fruit trees include the [common] grapevine similar to a slim woman, or wood-producing trees;

afterwards arrange the virgin soil for planting whatever you wish should prosper.

In the background let there be trees like the fig or any other which does no harm;

and any fruit tree which grows big, plant it in a confining basin so that its mature growth

may serve as a protection against the north wind without preventing the sun from reaching [the plants].

In the centre of the garden let there be a pavilion in which to sit, and with vistas on all sides,

but of such a form that no one approaching could overhear the conversation within and whereunto none could approach undetected.

Clinging to it let there be [rambler] roses and myrtle, likewise all manner of plants with which a garden is adorned.

And this last should be longer than it is wide in order that the beholder's gaze might expand in its contemplation.

As Dickie has shown, what Ibn Luyun describes is remarkably like the Patio de la Acqueia in the Generalife, especially as it has become known after recent excavations. It is also possible that some arrangement similar to the one implied by the poet must be imagined for the Court of the Myrtles. But Ibn Luyun's description is a very concrete one, reminiscent of the *Georgics* rather than of a paradisial garden. The point is of some importance, for it introduces into our understanding of the Alhambra the comparatively little studied theme of very practical and specific horticultural concerns. Through Ibn Luyun we may approach the gardens almost from the point of view of the gardener, or at least of a gentleman-gardener like Pliny. The still unresolved question is whether this was unique to Ibn Luyun or whether it was common in Andalusia and in the Muslim world at large. Its literary or archaeological expression is a rarity, but it implies in its loving practicality such obvious feelings and interests that it is difficult to imagine that it was not a prevalent concern in the fourteenth century and earlier. The feeling of sheer pleasure at seeing water in the midst of rich vegetation is inescapable in the ramps with channels of rapidly flowing water above the Generalife [60].

The second document leads to entirely different conclusions. It too is a poem, and it concerns the Fountain of the Lions [82 and 83]. It will be recalled that there is now general agreement that the lions themselves are probably eleventh-century and that the basin set over them was not made for them.[34] The basin itself is of the fourteenth century and carries this long poetical inscription:[35]

> *Blessed be He who gave to the Imam Muhammad [i.e. Muhammad V] abodes which grace by their perfection all abodes;*
> *or does not this bower [rawd] contain wonders like unto which God did not allow Beauty to find an equal.*
> *A sculpted monument, its veil of splendour consists of a pearl which adorns the environ with the diffusion of gems;*
> *silver melting which flows between jewels one like the other in beauty, white in purity.*
> *A running stream evokes the illusion of being a solid substance and one wonders which one is in truth fluid.*
> *Don't you see that it is the water which is running over the rim of the fountain, whereas it is the monument which offers long channels for the water;*

82. The Fountain of the Lions

83. *The Fountain of the Lions, detail*

    like one in love whose lids overflow with tears and who curbs the tears in fear of a slanderer.

    What else is it in truth but a mist which sheds forth from the fountain drenchings towards the lions?

    It [the fountain] resembles in this the hand of the caliph when it happens that it sheds forth supports towards the lions of the Holy War.

O thou who beholdest the lions whilst they are crouching, timidity
preventing them from becoming hostile;

O thou heir of the Helpers [of Muhammad, the Prophet] and thus
not through distant kin, a heritage of glory enabling you to raise even the
well-rooted [mountains],

God's blessing upon thee and mayest thou be blessed eternally to
reiterate celebrations and to wear down thine enemies.

This complex poem, probably by Ibn Zamrak, is full of fascinating references and rather uncomfortable hyperboles. For our purposes it has two important themes. One is that water is seen metaphorically as a solid substance made into a sculpted monument, or at least as giving the illusion of a solid monument; water, in other words, becomes a work of art, or at any rate the material substance for a work of art. The other theme is that of the fountain as the prince which supports the Lions of the Holy War. The monument itself, a water basin supported by animals, is of a common enough type with many known parallels,[36] but in the Alhambra it is provided with the specific meaning of royal victory, and, as so often in Islamic art, it is not the forms themselves which express this meaning but the writing put on them. A poem provides a fairly simple and traditional motif with iconographic specificity.

Yet matters are in reality even more complicated and more fascinating, thanks to Bargebuhr's discovery of an extraordinary poem by the Jewish poet of the eleventh century, Ibn Gabirol, who had been a protégé of the Jewish viziers, themselves the first builders on the Alhambra hill. The poem describes a palace. There is some doubt whether it is a real or an imaginary palace; Bargebuhr favours the former because the beginning of the poem refers to a setting strikingly similar to the Alhambra's, but in my judgement the poem as a whole appears more of a literary exercise.[37] But, whether real or imaginary, the palace is endowed with a very curious feature:

And there is a full 'sea', matching Solomon's Sea, yet not resting on
ox;

but there are lions, in phalanx on its rim, seeming to roar for prey, these whelps,

whose bosoms are like wells that gush spurts up from their mouths like streams.

And there are hinds embedded in the channels hollowed out as water spouts,

to sprinkle the plants in the beds and to shed on the lawns clear waters,

and also they water the myrtle garden; they sprinkle the tree-tops like clouds.

The fragrance is like perfume fragrance as if they were thurified with myrrh-incense.

Although the poet has sprinkled his verse with direct biblical quotations typical of this poetical genre, the key point of the passage is evident. In the palace there was a basin set on lions which is compared to the Brazen Sea in Solomon's Temple, which was set upon twelve oxen (1 Kings 7.23–6). Lions are frequently mentioned in the biblical text as well (1 Kings 7.29), and the throne overlaid with gold which was erected in honour of the Queen of Sheba had twelve lions (1 Kings 10.18–20). Of course it might be thought quite natural for a Jewish poet to make some biblical comparison in his description of any monument or event of importance, but in this instance what appears a simple literary metaphor acquires particular importance because the poem itself is quite unique in its time and because it involves Solomon, the King-Prophet who had become in medieval Jewish and Muslim legend the prince *par excellence*. To limit ourselves at this stage to his association with water and gardens, a few examples may suffice. Solomon is supposed to have built a golden garden with gilt likenesses of all trees, and God made it so that each golden tree produced fruits tasting like fruits from natural trees.[38] When Solomon met the Queen of Sheba, he created a floor of glass which was so much like water that the Queen lifted her robe to walk on it, thinking it was a pool.[39] These or related stories found architectural or artistic expression. The Fatimid caliphs, for instance, if we are to believe the surviving descriptions of their private treasures, had miniature, toylike gardens with gilded trees, animals, bodies of water, and barges. According to literary sources, the imperial palaces of the caliphs in Baghdad and their Constantinopolitan counterparts were provided with life-size artificial trees and animals; the peculiar floors of private ninth-century palaces of Raqqah in Syria, with water-like transparent glass mosaic cubes, may have sought to imitate the floor created for the Queen of Sheba.[40] The Crusaders copied this motif in one of their palaces in the Levant,[41] and it is possible that the representations of trees in early mosques like Damascus [78] or in palaces, like the late eleventh-century one in Bougie in Algeria described in a contemporary poem,[42] are further examples (though no doubt modified by other traditions too) of strikingly set-out water and beautiful gardens as translations in their own time of the all-pervading myth of a Solomonic palace.

We shall return later to several further aspects of this mythology. At this stage the point is that the Fountain of the Lions and the garden which originally surrounded it can be and were understood in their time on three different levels. They were very practical means to adorn a mansion, they were symbols of the prince's power and victory, and they were re-creations of a luxurious setting associated with Solomon. It is more difficult to establish the degree of formal consciousness the Muslim fourteenth century in Granada had of each one of these aspects; it should be stressed that only the second one, royal power and victory, is indubitably demonstrated by the poem on the basin. It cannot be *proved* that the very practical mood of Ibn Luyun's poem is applicable to the Alhambra, nor is it entirely clear whether the symbolic values which can be attributed to the Fountain of the Lions can be extended to the pools of the Court of the Myrtles, of the Partal, or of the Generalife. But the possibility of such symbolism is clearly there, and we shall see that it is confirmed by several other features of the Alhambra.

There is yet another aspect to a consideration of water and gardens in the Alhambra and it is a particularly important one for

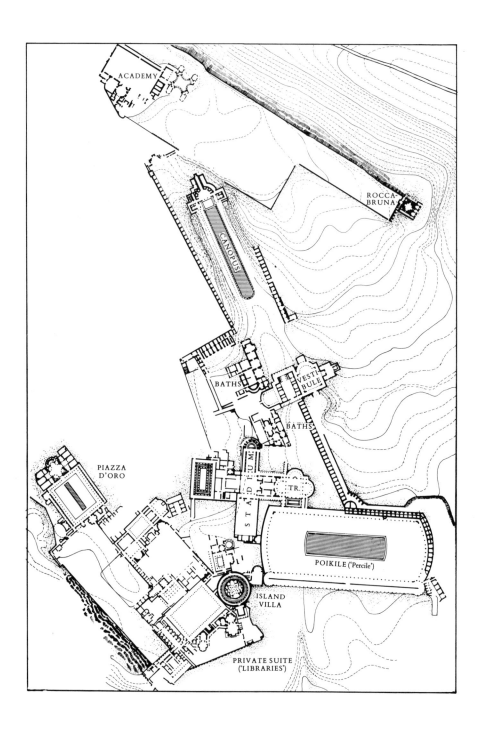

ACADEMY

ROCCA-
BRUNA

CANOPUS

BATHS

VESTI-
BULE

BATHS

PIAZZA
D'ORO

S
T
A
D
I
U
M

TR.

POIKILE ('Percile')

ISLAND
VILLA

PRIVATE SUITE
('LIBRARIES')

84. Tivoli, Hadrian's villa

our attempt to set the Alhambra in its historical and typological perspective. The physical relationship between fancy or practical buildings and water in gardens is a characteristic component of the *villa*, either the *villa rustica* or the *villa urbana* transferring into the city the values of a countrified atmosphere. Regardless of its possibly more ancient origins in little-known Near Eastern gardens, it is in imperial Rome that the villa developed simultaneously as a practical form of agricultural endeavour and as an imperial pleasure place. In the latter instance, as in Hadrian's villa at Tivoli [84] or Piazza Armerina [85], official, symbolic, and private architectural elements are spread informally amid nature.[43] It has been frequently suggested that typologically and

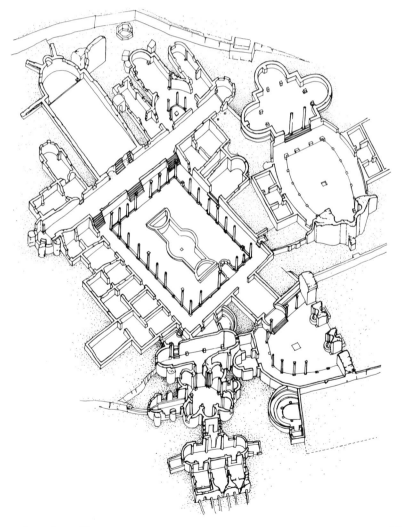

85. Piazza Armerina, villa

even formally the Roman villa was at the root of early Islamic châteaux in Syria.[44] What is perhaps less well realized is that Muslim Spain, far more consistently than other parts of the Islamic world, has preserved evidence for the existence of estates called *munyahs*, and in one instance *hayr*, in which gardens, pavilions, and living areas were found together and used for pleasure as well as for income.[45] Most of these examples are not later than the early eleventh century, and it may well be that their preservation was made more difficult by the politically unsettled conditions which followed the fall of the Umayyad caliphate in Cordova. But the memory of these heirs of the Roman villa in Spain remained in chronicles and stories; and, even though a formal relationship to the Alhambra is impossible to demonstrate in the absence of archaeological evidence, the garden villa with direct Roman roots is yet another facet of the architectural, formal, and ideological background of the Nasrid monument.

THE ALHAMBRA AND THE FAITH

A third component of the Alhambra is the faith of Islam. Its obvious architectural expression is the mosque. The large public mosque of the Alhambra 'city' has disappeared; but it has been proposed, on the basis of old descriptions, that it was not a very large one and that it had three naves.[46] The ruins of another mosque have been preserved in the forecourts west of the Mexuar; its small size, its minaret (if the neighbouring square tower is correctly interpreted), and its odd position in relationship to the rest of the building are all difficult to explain. Only a detailed study of its foundations could demonstrate whether it was an afterthought, added on to earlier buildings, or a part of the original building breaking up the symmetry of the architectural composition. For the two other oratories, near the Mexuar and beyond the Partal, the canonical requirement of orientation towards Mekkah was artfully adapted to the outer walls, and the eccentricity of the mosques' axes in relation to other parts of the palace is hardly visible.

The presence of such small oratories in or near major formal units of a palace is fully in the tradition of Muslim palaces since Khirbat al-Mafjar's small mosque inside the main residential part of the palace [86][47]; and it is comparable to the small private

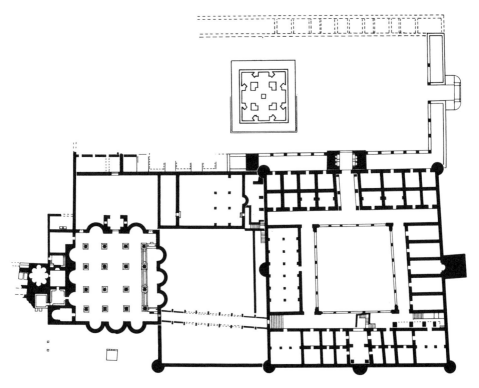

86. Khirbat al-Mafjar, plan

chapels of late medieval secular buildings in western Christendom. A secular atmosphere is characteristic of these oratories, for they share the decorative techniques and designs of other parts of the palaces. The oratory near the Mexuar in the Alhambra is almost like a balcony with openings on to the valley below – in contrast to the normal Muslim tradition for the holy place to be a closed building secluded from its environment. The princely elegance and the smallness of the oratories identify them as private buildings for restricted use only, but it is curious to note that the one near the Partal has a large number of Koranic quo-

tations (II, 239, and II, 80–83) that are typical of mosque decoration. One may wonder whether the reason why the iconography of inscriptions is correct in only one of the mosques is that
there was some difference in use between the two or whether the
explanation is simply that the inscriptions from the lower oratory
have disappeared.

The only other architectural element with an apparently
specific Islamic connotation is the Gate of Law, the main entrance
to the Alhambra from the south. Its name is rare in the nomenclature of city gates; the only other known instances occur in
Morocco.[48] An acknowledgement of the name's rarity appears
clearly in the beginning of its inscription, which says in effect that
Yusuf I ordered the construction of this gate 'to be called' or
'so-called' Gate of the *Shari'ah*. Several explanations have been
proposed for this name, the most common being that it was the
place where justice was administered, either actual sessions of
tribunals or executions and punishments. Since the practice of
providing justice at a city's gate is not a particularly Muslim one
and since it is exceedingly rare for a gate be named after an
abstract concept, Lévi-Provençal proposed that in this particular
context the word *shari'ah* must be understood in the restricted
western Islamic sense of an area reserved for major religious
holidays, a type of area which elsewhere in the Muslim world is
generally called a *musalla*. To name a gate according to what lies
outside it is a common enough practice, and enough evidence
exists to show that justice was at times carried out near *musallas*.
So there can be little doubt that Lévi-Provençal's explanation is
the one which best meets all requirements of the normal Muslim
nomenclature. The fact that western Islam seems to have provided divine Law, the cornerstone of orthodox Islam, with a
physical setting is an illustration of the orthodox formalism which
characterized so much of Muslim culture in the Maghrib. Its
appearance in the major monument of Nasrid Spain demon-
strates the dynasty's attachment to conservative *sunni* doctrines,
at least in external appearances.

In addition to the oratories and to the only slightly more problematic south gate, the faith of Islam appears in a number of Koranic quotations, usually with very specific meanings, as we have seen and shall see again later, or in a series of formulas which we have called 'redundant'. And it is true indeed that the endless repetition of 'Benediction', 'There is no Victorious One but God', 'Power is to God', and any number of other expressions, varying in length but rarely in sense, seems a rather meaningless feature to which it is difficult or incorrect to attribute any definite significance. Such inscriptions are frequent throughout Islamic architecture; for instance, at the other end of the Muslim world most of the major tile inscriptions of Timurid monuments in eastern Iran or Central Asia have, as a sort of counterpoint to the main historical or religious statement, the endless repetition, in a different colour (often red or ochre), of 'Power is to God' or some similar utterance.[49] Yet to consider all of them as meaningless and purely 'ornamental' is perhaps to misunderstand a very profound characteristic of medieval and especially late medieval Islamic culture. Repetitive though they may be, these inscriptions are constant reminders of the Muslim view of a unique God in Whom all reality resides; they illustrate the basic substratum of the faith, like crosses or other commemorative monuments on country roads in many Christian lands. Their presence in secular and palatial surroundings is in no way surprising, for Islam, as is well known, saw no separation between the holy life and daily life, and whatever happened in these buildings was always felt to be in the presence of the only permanent existence, that of God. In this sense, the whole building of the Alhambra is permeated with a deeply Muslim sense of a permanent presence of the divine, not as an agent in human affairs, nor as a witness requiring certain marks of respect or certain modes of behaviour (except in the oratories), but simply as the unavoidable possessor of all creation and of all time. It is through the repetitive litany of a small number of pious formulas that this aspect of the faith was made visible.

THE ALHAMBRA AND ROYAL SYMBOLS
AND CEREMONIES

Our discussion so far has suggested that some of the most obvious attributes of the Alhambra – its fortified exterior, its various uses of water, its repetitive references to God – can be interpreted in a number of ways, from very simple human or Islamic cultural needs to highly complex expressions of princely power which can be related to ancient and medieval princely traditions. But the official or private ceremonial function expected in a palatial establishment has not as yet been clarified. Traditional explanations are that the Court of the Myrtles with the two halls at its northern end and the more complex group of halls around the Court of the Lions served these purposes, but, apart from the argument that the Hall of the Ambassadors was used for the reception of dignitaries – and we have already seen (pp. 66–71) how tenuous the argument really is – very little has been brought out to indicate more precisely how these rooms were used and what was the difference in function between the two complexes of the Lions and of the Myrtles.[50] The suggestion that one complex was for winter use and the other for the summer makes no sense at all, for neither complex shows any consideration for climatic variation. To see them as the work of two successive princes competing with each other reflects a common enough characteristic of dynastic palaces, but the theory is weakened by the fact that Muhammad V redecorated so much in the earlier complex of Yusuf I; in his time at least, the whole of the Alhambra was used in some fashion or other. A more plausible explanation is that the complex of the Lions has a more private and restricted character than that of the Myrtles; through the Mirador de la Daraxa it overlooked the presumed private living quarters of the whole ensemble. A progression from public to private is logical enough in a palace – and is formally suggested in the Alhambra by the increasing luxury of interior arrangements. But, even if we can rank the two complexes from the points of view of privacy and accessibility, no real explanation emerges for their actual use.

Furthermore, why would it have been necessary under Muhammad V but not under Yusuf I to have groups of halls of varying degrees of privacy? Or did the complex of the Lions replace some other building?

In fact, there is as yet no satisfactory explanation of the function of the most impressive buildings of the Alhambra; and, what is far worse, there are no adequate archaeological parallels or literary references to enable us to imagine life in these complexes or to explain them through better-documented examples. A succession of separate units of varying decorative intensity does occur in Central Asian palaces of the eleventh and twelfth centuries (for example, Ghazni, Tirmidh, and Lashkari Bazar [71]), or Iraqi palaces of the eighth and ninth centuries (such as Kufah [87] and Samarra) or North African ones (such as Ashir [65] or the

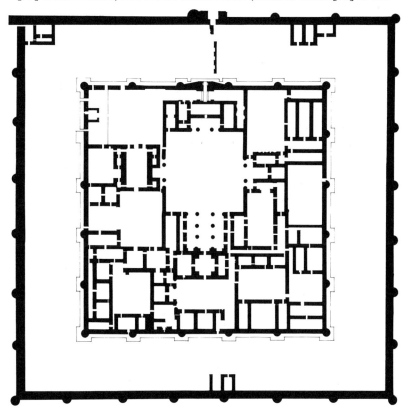

87. Kufah, palace, plan

Qal'ah of the Beni Hammad [77]), but in all these examples we are faced with two possibilities.[51] Either one hall or complex dominates all others by its form or decoration and can therefore be interpreted as a formal throne-room or reception hall; or else the internal evidence is too limited to justify any reconstruction of life and ceremonies. The latter are in fact poorly known from literary sources, and studies devoted to Abbasid, Fatimid, or Mamluk ceremonies have until now failed to relate them successfully to a known architecture.[52]

A more fruitful comparative approach would be to relate the Alhambra to later rather than earlier examples. The Ottoman complex at Topkapi in Istanbul, for instance, consists of a succession of pavilions and halls of different periods rather haphazardly planned in the midst of gardens, and we are reasonably well informed about the institution's ceremonies and life. [53] But two features of the Ottoman parallel weaken its usefulness. One is that too much is known about it, from kitchens to ceremonial rooms, and it becomes almost impossible to transfer such precise information to the very partially documented Alhambra. The other feature is that, however many traditional Islamic and Near Eastern aspects the Topkapi may have preserved, it belongs to another epoch and is not really a medieval palace complex. Furthermore, it was the imperial centre of a powerful dynasty, and, like Fathepur Sikri in Mughal India, it was on an utterly different scale, not necessarily in size but in intent and effect.

The monuments of the third late Muslim empire, the Persian empire of the Safavids, are perhaps closer to the Alhambra. In Isfahan the succession of brilliant pavilions like the Chehel Sutun (Forty Columns) [88] or the Hesht Behesht (Eight Paradises), set in gardens and separated from the rest of the city by the formal entrance-palace of the Ali Qapu [89], does bear some typological, if not stylistic, relationship to the Alhambra. Most of our information about the uses of these buildings derives from western travellers, from miniatures, and occasionally from decoration.

88. Isfahan, Chehel Sutun

89. Isfahan, Ali Qapu

On the whole these monuments were for pleasure and, even if formal affairs of state were also transacted in them and foreign envoys were officially received there, the dominant mood was that of a sensuously exciting setting.[54] The forms of the Safavid buildings are different from those of the Alhambra, but the idea that the principal objective of a princely establishment was to give physical pleasure rather than simply to provide a succession of official rooms with strictly practical purposes can serve as an explanation for the Spanish monument as well. It was already the dominant idea behind the early Islamic châteaux of Syria and Transjordan such as Khirbat al-Mafjar [73, 75 and 76], and even if we lose the thread of its development after the eighth century because of the lack of excavated monuments, we could simply conclude that there was no conscious and specific purpose or use to the main units of the Alhambra. Hidden and secluded, they were simply beautiful forms which provided pleasure for whatever activity may have taken place in them, just as a beautiful plate enhances the sensuousness of eating. That this kind of physical concern is deeply ingrained in Islamic art is a point to which we shall return in conclusion. At this stage in our search for the meanings and uses of the Alhambra, we may simply conclude that there was none, other than sensuous satisfaction, and that attempts to relate the various courts and rooms to specific activities or to explain the building in concrete historical terms contradict the tradition to which it belongs.

Yet it is in fact possible to propose a symbolic and even ceremonial explanation of the main buildings of the Alhambra by analysing their inscriptions. While it cannot be claimed that this explanation is complete and definitive, it is based on contemporary evidence, on texts specifically chosen for the decoration of these complexes.

Let us begin with the inscription found in the portico preceding the Sala de la Barca:

Blessed be He who has entrusted you with the command of His servants and who through you has exalted [the world of] Islam in benefits and favours;

and how many infidel lands did you reach in the morning only to become the arbiter of their lives in the evening!

You put on them the yoke of captives so that they appear at your doorstep to build palaces in servitude;

you conquered Algeciras by the sword and opened a gate which had [until then been] denied to our victory. . .

O son of eminence, prudence, courage and generosity, who has risen above the most brilliant stars,
you have risen on the horizon of your kingdom with mercy to dissipate the shadows of tyranny,
you have secured the branches from the blowing wind and you have frightened the stars in the vault of heaven;
if the flickering stars tremble, it is from fear of you, and if the branches of the willow bend, it is to give you thanks.

In characteristic hyperbolic style, this panegyric poem celebrates a particular victory, the taking of Algeciras in 1369, and uses two series of images about Muhammad V, nature glorifying him and the heavens in fear of him. The two small niches at the entrance of the Sala de la Barca contain the following poem:

I am [like] a bride in her nuptial attire, endowed with beauty and perfection.
Contemplate [this] ewer to understand the full truth of my statement;
look as well at my crown and you will find it similar to the crown of the new moon;
Ibn Nasr [Muhammad V] is the sun of this heaven in splendour and in beauty;
May he remain forever in [this] high position without fearing the time of sunset. . .

The rest of the poem, on the left niche, picks up again the point that the niche held a jar of water with the rather charming image of a jar in use being like a man in prayer, and ends with standardized praise of the prince. Most of the poem is quite concrete and specific in meaning, although it is probable that there was in it a word-play on *ibriq*, 'ewer', and *tabriq*, 'to provide with brilliance'. But its more important features are, first of all, that the part of the building on which it is found is describing itself and, second, that it introduces a new image, that of architecture as a bride. There was yet another poem in the Sala de la Barca; it disappeared over a century ago but, from the translation which has been preserved,[55] it seems to have been a rather uninspired royal panegyric.

The Hall of the Ambassadors is provided with an unusual number of inscriptions. At the entrance itself we find: 'Praise be to God; remove from Yusuf all effects of the evil eye with five statements', the latter being probably a reference to prayers. This is followed by a Koranic quotation: 'Say: I take refuge in the Lord of Dawn'; how much of the *surah* XCI (from which this passage is taken) actually followed is unclear from existing records, and the inscription itself survives only in part, but it is important to remember that this *surah* is a most impressive statement of cosmic power.[56] Above these quotations it is once again the building, or rather the niche for a water jug, which is speaking; and the themes of resplendence, the bride, and the practical wonders of water reappear.

Under the cupola of the hall one finds, apparently in its entirety, *surah* LXVII of the Koran, the *surah* of the Kingdom, whose first five verses are of central importance:

Blessed is He in whose hand is the Kingdom, He is powerful over everything, Who created death and life, that He might try you which of you is fairest in works; and He is the All-Mighty, the All-Forgiving, Who created seven heavens one upon another. Thou seest not in the creation of the All-Merciful any imperfection. Return thy gaze; seest thou any fissure? Then return thy gaze again, and again, and thy gaze comes back to thee dazzled, aweary. And We adorned the lower heaven with lamps, and made them things to stone Satans; and We prepared for them the chastisement of the Blaze.

It is rather strange that only Nykl (in 1936) and later Bargebuhr realized that it is precisely the seven heavens of the Koranic quotation which are represented in the decoration of the ceiling with its six rows of stars and its central small cupola [33].[57] The recent discovery of inscribed wooden panels providing some information about colours and shapes may lead to a more precise understanding of the geometry used in these representations, but the full exploitation of this document and of a series of new measurements is still in progress.[58]

Around the arch over the central alcove on the northern side of the hall, exactly in front of the entrance, there is the following inscription (*surah* XCIII of the Koran):

In the name of God the Compassionate, the Merciful, may God bless our Lord Muhammad and his people and grant him salvation. Say: I take refuge with the Lord of Daybreak, from the evil of what He has created, from the evil of darkness when it gathers, from the evil of the women who blow on knots, from the evil of an envier when he envies.

Then inside the alcove itself, at eye level, there is a poem; it is to be noted that only this central alcove, which is more elaborately decorated than any other, is provided with a poem rather than a redundant formula. The poem reads as follows:

You received from me morning and evening salutations of blessing, prosperity, happiness, and friendship;
   this is the high dome and we [presumably the alcoves] are its daughters; yet I have distinction and glory in my family;
   I am the heart amidst [other] parts [of the body], for it is in the heart that resides the strength of soul and spirit;
   my companions may be the signs of the zodiac in its [the cupola's] heaven, but to me only and not among them is the Sun of nobility;
   for my lord, the favourite [of God], Yusuf, has decorated me with the clothes of splendour and of glory without vestments;
   and he has chosen me as the throne of his rule; may his eminence be helped by the Lord of light, of the divine throne and see.

These verses clearly indicate that Yusuf I used the central alcove for his throne; but, more important, they strengthen the cosmic meaning of the room. Below the seven heavens of the central dome lies the earthly rule of the king, and his abode is more spectacular than that of the other stars or signs of the zodiac. The idea of a throne-room as a microcosm is not new, and we shall return shortly to some of its historical implications, but there are two aspects of the means by which the idea is expressed which are particularly important. One is that much of it is done through Koranic quotations, and that poetry appears almost as a sort of paraphrase of or elaboration on Koranic themes. The other point is that several secondary themes run through these inscriptions. One is the theme of an almost magical purification of the hall from danger: both at the entrance and over the axial alcove there are incantations to keep away temptations and evil. One may wonder whether this does not reflect some very specific, individual concern of Yusuf I or of his time, but what this concern or mood may have been can at this stage only be matters for speculation. Another theme is the more common cliché of the bride as a symbol of perfection; a third is the more specific one of power and victory. The latter, however, usually derives from additions made by Muhammad V.

If we turn to the complex of the Lions, the documentation is simpler because it is entirely of Muhammad V's time, but it is in some ways more complicated to interpret properly. The court itself has few inscriptions, except for redundant ones and the inscription on the basin of the fountain which has already been discussed. Only one of the redundant formulas is different from the norm found all over the palace. It occurs above those capitals in the portico which are closest to the entrance: 'Victory, protection, and an obvious conquest to our lord Abu Abdallah, Commander of the Faithful; glory to our lord, may God protect his rule and strengthen his victory.' The smaller rooms to the east are devoid of significant inscriptions, but the Hall of the Two Sisters contains Ibn Zamrak's poem, parts of which are repeated in the Hall of the Abencerrajes across the court:[59]

> I am the garden appearing every morning with adorned beauty;· contemplate my beauty and you will be penetrated with [its] understanding;
>
> I excel through the generosity of my lord the iman Muhammad for all who come and go;
>
> how excellent is your beautiful building, for it certainly surpasses all others by the decree of the stars!

How many joyful solaces for the eyes are to be found in it; in it even the dreamer will renew the objects of his desire!

The hands of the Pleiads will spend the night invoking God's protection in their favour and they will awaken to the gentle blowing of the breeze.

In here is a cupola which by its height becomes lost from sight; beauty in it appears both concealed and visible.

The constellation of Gemini extends a ready hand [to help it] and the full moon of the heavens draws near to whisper secretly to it.

And the bright stars would like to establish themselves firmly in it rather than to continue wandering about in the vault of the sky.

Were they to remain in its antechambers they would outstrip the handmaidens in serving you in such a way as to cause you to be pleased with them.

It is no wonder that it surpasses the stars in the heavens, and passes beyond their furthest limits.

For it is before your dwelling that it has arisen to perform its service, since he who serves the highest acquires merits thereby.

In it the portico has exceeded [the utmost limits] of beauty, while thanks to it the palace has come to compete in beauty with the vault of heaven.

With how many a decoration have you clothed it in order to embellish it, one consisting of multicoloured figured work which causes the brocades of Yemen to be forgotten!

And how many arches rise up in its vault supported by columns which at night are embellished by light!

You would think that they are the heavenly spheres whose orbits revolve, overshadowing the pillar of dawn when it barely begins to appear after having passed through the night.

The capitals [of the columns] contain all sorts of rare wonders so that proverbs [about them] fly in all directions and become generally known.

In it there is burnished marble whose light has shone and thus illuminated the darkest shadows remaining in the gloom.

When they are illuminated by the rays of the sun you would think that they are made of pearls by reason of the quantity of celestial bodies in them.

Nor have we observed any palace higher in its lookout spots, clearer in its horizons, or ampler in its halls of assembly.

Moreover we do not know of any other garden more pleasant in its freshness, more fragrant in its surroundings, or sweeter in the gathering of its fruits.

[The garden] gives double satisfaction for the amount which the judge of beauty imposed on it [as a fine].

For if the hand of the breeze fills it with [silver] dirhams of light, he is satisfied by its [payment].

Yet [in surplus] the [gold] dinars of the sun fill the enclosure of the garden filtering through its branches, leaving it embellished. . .

On the basis of textual evidence, Cardenas and Gallego y Burin suggested that this was once followed by a final verse: 'Between victory and me there is the noblest relationship; it is in fact an identity.'[60] Since only some twenty of the poem's 146 verses are quoted and since they are not in the order in which they were written, it is reasonable to conclude that the choice was made consciously and that they have a precise iconographic meaning.

While many uncertainties of detail remain about the poem as a whole, none exist about its major themes and images: the garden, the cupola to which heavenly bodies come, brilliance of colours and of effects, victory. Throughout, however, as in the Hall of the Ambassadors, the main emphasis is on heavenly and cosmic themes, and this makes it possible to identify the dome of the Hall of the Two Sisters as another instance of the classical motif of the dome of heaven.[61] Instead of complex images (as in most of the antique and late antique examples collected by Lehmann) or the wood inlays of the Hall of the Ambassadors, the technique used here was the very different one of muqarnas combinations of small units in three dimensions (discussed in the next chapter). As was mentioned with respect to the Hall of the Ambassadors, there is nothing new or peculiar about a palatial dome with cosmic symbols, and, although unfortunately our knowledge of the motif is mostly literary, its commonness, especially in western Islamic architecture of previous centuries,[62] makes its presence in the Alhambra hardly surprising. The only question is why there was a need for two such heavenly halls in one palace.

There is another peculiarity in the dome of the Two Sisters and its companion on the other side of the court. Once again it was Bargebuhr who first noticed it, although he came to his conclusion in a different way from the one we shall propose here. An unusual aspect of the cosmic imagery in Ibn Zamrak's poem is that the celestial bodies of the cupola move in their orbits and that the hall itself changes in appearance by day and by night. It is as though the cupola was understood as a rotating one, reflecting the daily cycle of light and darkness and the changing positions of constellations. It may be that this is not merely a literary image, for it can be argued that the very structure of the cupola [50] is an attempt to represent a rotating cupola. Here, instead of the primarily two-dimensional and schematic symbolizations of the Hall of the Ambassadors, we meet with a surface which is broken up in what appears to be an almost infinite number of facets, at an angle from each other. The dome is lit by windows set below it, and as the source of light, sun or moon, changes its location, different combinations of facets are illuminated, giving an illusion of rotation. In fact this rotation would be an illustration of a pre-Galilean conception of the sun rotating round the earth. Whether or not this last point was reached consciously in all its detail is perhaps debatable, but the central conception of the heavens – always different yet always the same – corresponds to a medieval vision of the universe. We shall see in the next chapter that the surface decoration of parts of the Alhambra can be similarly interpreted as a representation of fundamental rhythms of the universe, but since those designs are more common than the structure of the domes and lack immediate literary commentary, they belong to a different, more artisanal level of consciousness.

To interpret this Alhambra dome as a rotating heavenly cupola is historically justifiable. The poem of Ibn Gabirol from which we have already (pp. 127–8) discussed one passage also contains the following:

> The buildings [of the palace] are built and decorated with openwork, intaglios and filigrees,
> paved with marble slabs and alabaster – I cannot count its many gates.

The doors are like those of the ivory mansions reddened by palatial algum woods.

And there are windows, transparent above them, skylights where dwell the luminous planets.

The dome is like the Palanquin of Solomon hung above the glories of the chambers,

that rotates in its gyre, shining like opals and sapphire and pearls;

this it is in the daytime, while at dusk it looks like the sky whose stars form constellations. [63]

Thus eleventh-century Jewish poetry about a real or imaginary palace not only speaks of a rotating dome of heaven but also associates it with Solomon, the King-Prophet. There is no obvious biblical parallel for the motif, as there is for the fountain supported on animals. Instead it was a group of monuments illustrating royal myths, probably of Hellenistic origin, which found their way into the Solomonic legend. Discussed at great length by L'Orange,[64] this group includes the Domus Aurea of Nero in Rome, with its rotating cosmic dome, and the throne of Khosro II, where the emperor was represented in 'the cupola of his palace, as though enthroned in heaven, and around him were the sun, the moon and the stars. . .and machines were set up to throw drops like rain and to make noise like thunder.'[65] Although the date of the formation of the myth of the rotating dome and the manner of its development are still very unclear, it was certainly in existence by the early Middle Ages. In literary form it appears in the Muslim world in tenth-century Iran with the national epic of the *Shahnameh* and with Tha'alibi's history of Persia. Occasional features seemingly related to the myth occur in a number of earlier monuments, for instance in the eighth-century palace of Khirbat al-Mafjar, with winged horses supporting one cupola [90], and Atlantes and figures possibly derived from representations of stars and planets holding up another [91].[66] It is, however, difficult to know whether the early Islamic examples are entirely conscious cosmic symbols or merely borrowings derived for ornamental purposes only from earlier artistic traditions.[67] Similarly we cannot be certain that urban palaces or

90. *Khirbat al-Mafjar, reconstruction of small room*

91. *Khirbat al-Mafjar, Atlantes and other figures*

pavilions from the ninth to the eleventh centuries with such names as Palace of the Throne of Paradise or Palace of the Pleiads were conscious illustrations of the myth of the heavenly palace,[68] although a very curious text does suggest that effects of rotation through light were attempted in the tenth-century palace in Madinah al-Zahra mentioned earlier. In this instance, however, the effect was created not by architecture but by moving back and forth a basin filled with quicksilver.[69]

What seems clear is that at a certain moment various themes – memories of ancient monuments and ceremonies, folk imagination around standing ruins and other remains from old, practical ceremonies, types of design – all coalesced in more or less coherent form around Solomon. They appear in Jewish legends which are impossible to date, just as it is still impossible to know whether the phenomenon was first an Islamic one, seeking to adapt to its own symbolic system a newly discovered life of princely luxury and newly acquired memories of ancient kings, or whether it is another instance of the impact of medieval Jewish ideas on the dominant Muslim culture, or whether the theme of Solomon as the perfect king was already in existence in Justinian's time. In whatever way these questions are eventually resolved, it seems evident that from the moment of the establishment of the Muslim empire, a Solomonic consciousness grew, and, sooner or later, slowly or rapidly, an automatic association with Solomon developed for all themes, myths, and ideas which pertained to the life of the prince and to its setting. As a result, from the Maghrib to Central Asia, major ruins became known as 'thrones' or other attributes of Solomon.[70]

In fact, Solomonic association became almost a subconscious aspect of the culture, and in the Alhambra the inscriptions do not refer to the King-Prophet at all. By the fourteenth century in Andalusia, the creation of a garden for a prince with a fountain surrounded by handsomely decorated buildings can be considered as an automatic gesture without compelling symbolic meaning; the myth may have become a cliché. Yet we may prefer not to consider the complex of the Lions in this way. For how can we explain the decision to cover these rooms with inscriptions, often original ones, other than as an attempt to annotate the building, to provide it with specific explanations wherever they could easily be seen? This decision is interesting because it seems to correspond psychologically to a moment of revival, to a time when there was some uncertainty whether forms would be properly understood in the way in which the patrons wanted them to be understood. The phenomenon occurs fairly often in provincial or late schools of religious or mythological painting, where a written legend is thought necessary to explain a visual motif which at another time or in another setting would have been obvious. In this respect the main buildings of the Alhambra reflect something of the artificial traditionalism which we have suggested characterizes much of late Islamic Spain.

But, while we can propose that the two major complexes of the Alhambra are domes of heaven set in enclosed paradisial gardens and that they reflect, in Solomonic terms, a complex mythology of princely life and princely settings going back at least to classical antiquity, we are still left with the related questions why they were built and what took place in them. For the Hall of the Ambassadors the explanation as a throne-room seems demonstrated, but not, as has hitherto been believed, for the formal reception of foreign envoys, but rather as a brilliant setting for royal presence. Yusuf I's creation of such an elaborate reception hall near living quarters and a bath makes reasonable, almost prosaic sense, the complex symbolism of one hall notwithstanding. But the actual purpose of Muhammad V's work is still problematic, in as much as he reworked so much of his predecessor's complex.

Once again it is the inscriptions that may lead us to an explanation, albeit a tenuous one. We have noted frequently that on almost all his creations Muhammad V referred to victory; this was so in his inscriptions in the Court of the Myrtles, on the Fountain of the Lions, on the columns of the Court of the Lions, even in the bath, and possibly at the end of the poem in the Hall of the Two Sisters. And there is one more monument to add to the series. It is the Puerta del Vino [56 and 57], the curious gate in the middle of the Alhambra which in its shape and location does not make any military or defensive sense and which was also built by Muhammad V. Its inscription contains the first verses of the Koranic *surah* of Victory (*surah* XLVIII): 'Surely We have given thee a manifest victory, that God may forgive thee thy former and thy latter sins, and complete His blessings upon thee on a straight path, and that God may help thee with mighty help.' When read together, these inscriptions suggest that Muhammad V's buildings were in effect triumphal constructions commemorating his two successes, his return to the throne in 1362 and especially his taking of Algeciras in 1369, after which the town was entirely destroyed. As one of the relatively rare Muslim victories over Christians in the fourteenth century, it was celebrated with unique brilliance.

It is quite easy to see the Puerta del Vino, with its windows above the gateway and its location in the middle of the Alhambra compound, as a sort of triumphal arch. As part of the celebrations Yusuf's older palace would have been redecorated and victory inscriptions added, while the central monument to the reconquest was a new compound in which all the themes of the classical Islamic palace tradition were consciously re-created. In this sense, the Court of the Lions and its surrounding halls were not meant as settings for particular ceremonies or for any other court functions; they were to be a commemorative monument in honour of a victory, and would express, both formally and through the iconography of inscriptions, a complex ideology of princely themes going back to Khosro, Nero, and Solomon. And it is important to note that, next to poems of a more routine type celebrating the beauty of the place, the Mirador de la Daraxa overlooking the presumed living quarters of the palace still proclaimed the glory of Muhammad V, the 'conqueror of cities'.[71]

There is something poignant in the thought that a ruler from a secondary dynasty in the collapsing Muslim culture of Spain should have created a monument so infused with literary and symbolic memories as the Alhambra and that this monument survived, while the masterpieces which in reality or in imagination served as its models are all gone. In itself this is not surprising, and it has a parallel in Constantinople, where the fourteenth-century Kahrie Cami has survived but not the imperial palaces or the great church of the Holy Apostles. If the Alhambra survived, however, it was not by accident but in part because its architecture and decoration had acquired a significance and a prestige which far outweighed the symbolic significance that had belonged to them at their inception. In later centuries Ferdinand and Isabella or Charles V could enjoy them and disregard their meanings because in large part their eyes and their minds were no longer attuned to understanding the deeper implications of the forms used in the Alhambra. When Philip II built the Escorial, he still sought to express biblical and imperial themes of old; but his vocabulary and language were such that the same or related ideas were incomprehensible to him in another idiom. Had he or his predecessors been able to understand them, they would probably not have preserved the Alhambra, whose deepest meanings are steeped in that late antique culture out of which all medieval traditions evolved. But to the Renaissance or even pre-Renaissance Christian, the only point of the Alhambra was its alien exoticism, not its close relationship to their common 'antique' past.

This chapter has sought to establish some of the coordinates by which the Alhambra can be understood as a monument of its own time and as the sum of a number of older traditions. Four themes were selected – fortress, water, faith, iconography – not because they are the only possible ones, but because they seemed at this stage in our knowledge to lend themselves best to possible conclusions and hypotheses. Three key conclusions should be brought out. One is that the Alhambra does not appear simply as an exciting setting for pleasure, as has so often been thought and written. It is in fact a strikingly and consciously learned monument, in which a sort of summary of medieval themes about princely ideology is made visible. Even if further research modifies, as it is bound to do, some of our specific hypotheses, the general point still remains that, as far as its meaning is concerned, the Alhambra fits naturally and easily into the typology of traditional Islamic palaces. Its concerns and its aims were not extraordinary at all. It is unique only in that it has been preserved. The main impetus for the building of the Court of the Lions and for the refurbishing of the rest of the Alhambra consisted, I suggest, in Muhammad V's desire to commemorate his successes, particularly his victory at Algeciras. It is more difficult to elucidate Yusuf I's motives in initiating the transformation of what had been a fortress-city surrounded by gardens, even though in our analysis his work did not have the typological originality of his successor's monuments. An additional key may be provided by the poetic inscriptions of the Tower of the Captive, one of the more strictly defensive towers on the north side of the Alhambra.[72] Beyond a number of common images, these inscriptions are diffused with official piety and with a sense of the prince's duty to protect and maintain an ancient Islamic and more concretely Arab tradition. Yusuf I, in his construction, especially in the Hall of the Ambassadors, sought to give dignity and strength to a dynasty now firmly established after the feudal battles of previous centuries. Muhammad V, whose life was more chequered and more complex, celebrated a rare victory with a magnificent monument. It may be inappropriate to compare the 'deep structure' of this development to that of Versailles under Louis XIV and Louis XV, or to the altarpiece at Pergamum in relation to the Parthenon frieze, but it is perhaps not unique in the history of monuments that the most brilliant, most learned, and most complex work of art was made possible by an older and more sober creation and was itself inspired by a relatively minor event.

The second conclusion is that, if we can propose explanations for the construction of most buildings in the Alhambra, it is very difficult to imagine what sort of life went on in most of them. We

92. *Niche for a water jar at the entrance to the Hall of the Two Sisters*

have seen how tenuous are the arguments for the use of the Mexuar as a council chamber, and indeed there is much doubt about the existence of council chambers in medieval Islam in general. In fact we can be certain only about the location of the throne in the Hall of the Ambassadors whenever the latter was used for formal purposes, about the uses of the bath, possibly about the location of living quarters, and probably about visits to and parties in the outer gardens. But for the rest, and especially for the compound of the Lions, we have no direct information nor even such details as chimneys, closets, furniture, and the like. The presence of water jars on either side of the hall preceding the Hall of the Ambassadors and at the entrance of the Hall of the Two Sisters [92] is the sum total of our practical knowledge of common, expected activities. It is quite remarkable that the same uncertainty surrounds many of the earlier Muslim palaces, such as the Umayyad group, where it is generally only through formal analogies of architectural elements with pre-Islamic uses of the same elements that conclusions or hypotheses can be reached. The lack of a coherent Book of Ceremonies, if one ever existed, is only part of the reason for this uncertainty, since ceremonies which can be described, as in middle Abbasid or Fatimid times, are far more difficult to visualize in a specific architectural context than their Byzantine counterparts or than the well-documented Ottoman or even late medieval Western practices. It may be, perhaps, that the medieval Islamic world never developed any specificity of meaning in their palace architecture and that all these buildings, whatever the reasons for their construction, were simply considered as settings for whatever life happened from time to time to take place in them. Even when one can propose a concrete explanation for the forms and immediate connotations of a princely monument, the monument itself did not reflect precise specifications of ceremonial or practical use, being intended merely as an elaborate shell for man to use as he saw fit. To the broader implications of this point we shall return in the last chapter.

Yet, leaving aside the queries and problems which arise in defining the Alhambra as a monument of Islamic civilization, a most remarkable conclusion about the palace is that so frequently explanatory parallels for it are not Islamic but classical. In part this conclusion reflects the overwhelming impact of the Roman imperial tradition throughout the Middle Ages in and around the Mediterranean. Practically contemporary with each other, Spalato and Piazza Armerina are third-century prototypes – or rather prefigurations – of the Alhambra, while the Domus Aurea of Nero or Hadrian's villa at Tivoli are its forefathers. But in another way our conclusion implies that the ideological components of secular art, most specifically of the art of princes, tended to be more universal than those of the faith, even if the forms which expressed these components were unique. It is within some kind of equilibrium between direct filiation with antiquity through Syrian and Cordovan examples of earlier centuries and a ubiquitous medieval vision of princely life in a concretely Muslim shape that the functions and meanings of the Alhambra must be understood.

Chapter 3

FORMS AND VALUES: ARCHITECTURE AND DECORATION

The style and quality of the Alhambra as a formal ensemble and as an inspiration for later, especially *mudejar*, architecture will be the subject with which we conclude this chapter. Our first concern, however, must be to define and explain the forms themselves under three headings: composition, elevation, decoration. Although mindful of the likelihood of a stylistic evolution from the works of Yusuf I in the early part of the fourteenth century all the way to the fifteenth-century halls in the Tower of the Captive, we have minimized these differences and concentrated on what can be assumed to have been done or used during the time of Muhammad V in the second half of the fourteenth century.

One last preliminary remark is pertinent. The division for purposes of analysis into composition, elevation, and decoration is partly one of convenience, for in our perception and probably also in the process of creation these categories are inextricably mixed with each other. But this is not entirely so, for the simple contemplation of the plan [endpaper] does not necessarily and automatically provide a clue to the nature of the elevations [29, 40 and 41], and most of the decoration could be removed and replaced by work in other techniques and by other designs. In other words, it is possible that in the Alhambra, in contrast to a Gothic cathedral or a Palladian villa, the monument's morphological structure consists of at least three parallel sets of terms. Each one has its own history, development, and origins; and the key aesthetic problem of the building is to determine the nature of the relationship between the three sets. Is the relationship syntactic, akin perhaps to the harmonic combinations of a musical composition in which very different instruments support each other more or less equally in some complex counterpoint? Or is one set dominant, like a voice or a single instrument utilizing the others for help or emphasis in expressing itself? Or does the monument consist of three entirely separate and independent formal systems? In seeking answers to these questions, we shall try to establish what may be called the 'dimension' of the building, in part the mood its forms create and in part the mood they demand of the viewer or the user. For, beyond the necessary coordinates of originality or lack thereof which are established by comparisons with other monuments, we must seek to define the ways in which the monument affects the senses: what has been rather frivolously called its 'dimension amoureuse'.[1]

COMPOSITION

It has long been established that the central compositional cell in the Alhambra is the rectangular court.[2] In the Cuarto Dorado, the Court of the Myrtles, the Court of the Lions, the earlier units west of the main palaces, and even in the Generalife, a central space open to the sky serves as the focus or axis around or along which all other features are arranged. There is nothing particularly original about a secular monument centred around a courtyard, and the composition as such belongs to so ancient and so ubiquitous a Mediterranean and Near Eastern tradition that no particular claim to originality can be claimed for the Alhambra at this level of generality, nor is it possible to specify its exact origins. The characteristic feature of a body of water, pool or fountain, in the centre of every one of the courts is perhaps less usual, but common enough in palaces, houses, and even mosques from early Islamic times onwards, so that its presence in the Alhambra is not surprising.

Around this cell with its body of water, a very small number of other compositional units is found. In the centre of every major axis there is a square room or, in the instance of the narrow sides of the Court of the Lions, a square pavilion. Most of these square units are preceded by a rectangular hall and frequently also by a portico. In the Cuarto Dorado complex a portico and a long hall are found alone, while on the west and east sides of the Court of the Lions the order is reversed: the square pavilion precedes rather than follows the long hall and the portico. It is also only in the complex of the Lions that a complete arcade goes round the whole open court. Square halls and long halls are almost always characterized by the presence of niches or alcoves, usually heavily decorated and serving either to frame the hall (as with the Sala de la Barca and the Hall of the Kings [45]) or to bring in light as well as to direct one's eyes – but not one's movements – to the outside (as in the Hall of the Ambassadors [31] and the Mirador de la Daraxa [51]). As Marçais demonstrated, the combination of portico–long hall–square hall is a direct descendant of Hellenistic and Vitruvian compositional elements, the *prostas* and the *oecus*, which, since Priene in Asia Minor, were typical units of house composition, the former serving as a means of passage (Marçais calls it an *anti-salle*) to the latter. The regional or other variations which occur in the development of this basic combination can only be sketched. It has been proposed that the series of private dwellings found in the eighth-century palace at Ukhaydir in Iraq [93] first exhibited the meeting of the portico-*prostas* with the vaulted form of the *eyvan*; that from that moment onwards there was an unbroken succession of houses and palaces employing all kinds of variations on this basic theme; and that it was in North Africa and eventually in the poorly preserved twelfth-century palace at Murcia in Spain [94][3] that the compositional system later found in the Alhambra was first crystallized.

The most interesting development in western Islamic secular architecture [65 and 77] is that the main square hall so frequently projects beyond the lines of the building's walls and amplifies the ubiquitous exterior defensive towers into lookouts. Concern for a dramatic view is not unique to western Islamic architecture. Although unknown in early Islamic monuments, it occurs in the

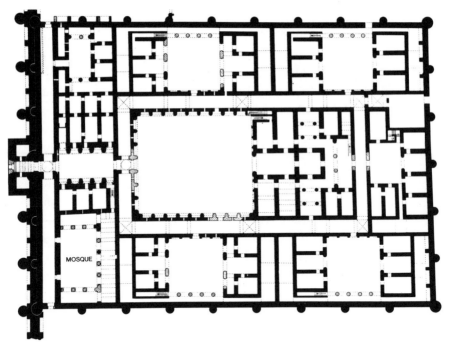

93. *Ukhaydir, plan*

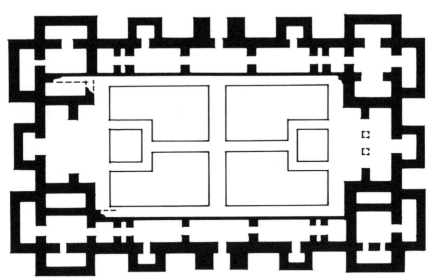

94. *Murcia, twelfth-century palace, plan*

twelfth-century palace at Lashkari Bazar in Afghanistan [71]. It also appears occasionally in pre-Islamic architecture, as in the second-century A.D. Palace of the Dux Ripae at Dura-Europos [95], where a whole side of the establishment was turned away from the court so as to take advantage of a spectacular view over the Euphrates.[4] Nevertheless, even if it was not uncommon, the use of towers is, in the Middle Ages, more typical of western Islam than of other regions.

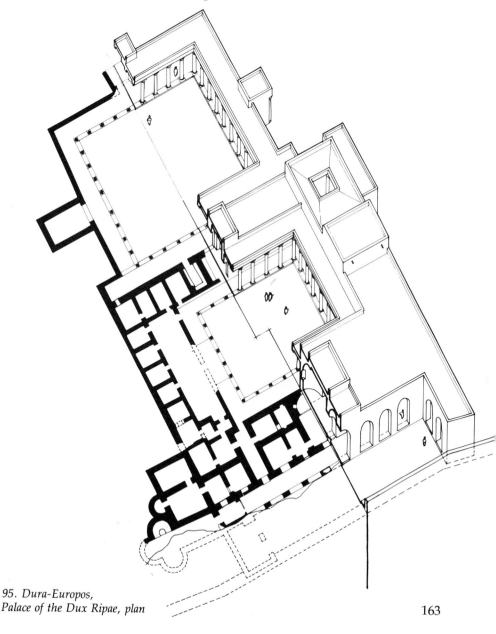

95. Dura-Europos,
Palace of the Dux Ripae, plan

Altogether the primary terms of the plan of the Alhambra are characteristic of a tradition going back to the architectural vocabulary of Hellenistic and Roman times, modified over the centuries by a number of peculiarly Near Eastern and Islamic features, like the use of towers and of water. While there is nothing so very surprising about this conclusion, it deserves emphasis because the relationship of Islamic architecture, especially in the West, to classical prototypes is too often forgotten. And possibly it was the direct impact of Roman triumphal arches and gates which led to the form and function of the Puerta del Vino.

Yet, beyond the simple level of identifying and enumerating compositional elements, there are two aspects of the planning of the Alhambra which show a far greater degree of originality and importance: the organization of the complex of the Lions and the definition of the point of view from which major compositions are to be seen.

The complex of the Lions is not a simple juxtaposition of separate units, as its immediate prototype in Murcia, and the complex of the Myrtles are, however well proportioned and studied the juxtaposition may be. It is in fact a very intricate complex in which the whole and its parts are unusually related to each other. One instance of this complexity has already been mentioned. The square pavilion on the short side of the court precedes the long hall and projects inward into the courtyard. This is the exact reverse of the usual order found on the longer sides. It illustrates a very interesting principle of Islamic decorative art rarely seen in architecture, that of making ornamental themes meaningful both positively and negatively within the same composition. In other words, the background of a design may also be seen as the main decorative motif.

Something quite different occurs in the Hall of the Two Sisters. This square room is surrounded on three sides by rectangular halls which transform the modular square into a larger one whose sides are approximately equal to the diagonal of the original square. This system of organic growth of a plan through what has been called dynamic squares has been determined as a characteristic means of development in Central Asian Islamic architecture.[5] Unfortunately only in Central Asia have adequate measurements been made for the elaboration of geometric planning principles. And, since it is highly unlikely that the Alhambra was influenced by Central Asia, we must conclude that it was a fairly common principle of composition throughout the Muslim world. We can only suggest its mathematical validity for the Hall of the Two Sisters, but there is little doubt about the transformation of the traditional simple square room into a self-generating module. The ultimate effect is that of a Chinese box, in which squares and rectangles create squares within squares and the unit as a whole is completed with a small projecting square, which, like a full stop, closes the unit off not with a wall but with a view to the outside world.

The Hall of the Abencerrajes, across the Court, is much simpler, but there also the dome-covered square appears in plan as a rectangular room with two deep rectangular recesses separated from the centre by a single columnar support. The square here seems to have been compositionally diluted rather than geometrically coherent, but this judgement may be corrected by a careful metrological investigation, so far unavailable for most of the monument.

Finally, the composition of the complex of the Lions sought to unify covered and open spaces with water channels and fountains. Beyond the iconographic meaning of these elements (discussed in the previous chapter), their point is at the same time to strengthen visually the main axes of the composition and to eliminate the contrast between covered and open areas. The two are in reality made to appear as a single space in which there occurs a continuous succession of different exposures to light, as we shall see in greater detail in discussing elevations. While the use of water as an axis unifying roofed and open spaces had already been suggested in Sicilian pavilions of the eleventh and twelfth centuries[6] and may have had much earlier Near Eastern origins, it is only in the Alhambra that it has been preserved in an elaborate form.

Altogether, the complex of the Lions is compositionally remarkable in that it sought to avoid the basically additive order of the complex of the Myrtles and of so much earlier palace architecture. It succeeded not by inventing new formal units of plan, but by elaborating the traditional, additive relationship between court, square and rectangular hall into the more cerebral relationship of self-generating modular units.

There is yet another, more general, area in which the Alhambra's compositions differ from their known models and illustrate a particularly characteristic feature of traditional aesthetics in Islamic architecture. With the one anomalous exception of the Cuarto Dorado [19 and 20], all units of the Alhambra are meant to be seen from their centre and not from the outside or through an elaborate façade. In the complex of the Myrtles [21 and 22], the main halls can be seen only from the court; in the complex of the Lions [38] or the Generalife [58–9], it is a sort of interior façade on the four sides of the court which introduces the covered areas beyond. In the instance of the Court of the Lions, the compositional principle can be defined as that of the Parthenon inside out. Such compositions are not peculiar to the Alhambra. The search for ways to diminish the contrast between covered and open areas is a characteristic of early Islamic mosque architecture,[7] and, while the architectural terms are quite different, the Masjid-e Jomeh in Isfahan in its twelfth- or fourteenth-century version[8] also shows an internal façade from which the rest of the building expands.

It is tempting to interpret this particular aspect of the Alhambra's composition as a wilful return to a traditional Islam-wide aesthetic of a vision of the architectural monument from the inside out. This would have been a rejection of a second and more recent development of the formal exteriorization of architectural monuments through elaborate portals, which began in Iran in the tenth century and dominated the city architecture of a town like

Cairo from the twelfth century onwards. But there is some danger in proposing a purely aesthetic choice as a source for the Alhambra's composition, for there may be a simpler explanation in the fact that, with the exception of the Umayyad palaces of the eighth century and to a smaller degree the Ali Qapu of seventeenth-century Isfahan [89], Islamic palaces and private dwellings tended to avoid any exterior expression of their interior brilliance. Thus the Alhambra's composition may simply illustrate a secular palace tradition rather than a more generalized Islamic aesthetic tendency of early times. At this stage of research into the principles of Islamic architectural composition it is not possible to choose between a consciously revivalist and a typically functional explanation of the Alhambra's planning principles. Both may have been involved.

ELEVATION

As has already been pointed out, and as is abundantly clear from sections through the Alhambra [29, 40, 41 and 96], the most characteristic features of the monument's elevation are the simplicity of its wall structure and the contrast between interior and exterior profiles. The latter are simple outlines of large square or polygonal masses, while the former are extraordinarily elaborate linear compositions. This contrast was achieved thanks to a striking difference between the treatment of walls and other supports on the one hand and ceilings and other means of covering space on the other.

There are only two kinds of support in the Alhambra, walls and columns. Walls are plain and hardly ever articulated. Their construction was never visible, for they were covered with plaster on the outside and with a flat decoration on the inside. They are pierced with openings which are either passageways, only very rarely provided with actual doors, or windows. Passageways or windows are always covered with a raised arch framed in a decorative unit, but these arches were rarely shown as structural

96. The Tower of the Infantas, section

units. Exceptions in the Cuarto Dorado [19 and 20] and in the entry into the Mexuar, with their suggestion of a flat rather than curved arch, occur only in those openings which were provided with doors. Whether the latter are to be explained by some technical advantage or by formal tradition, the main point is that the walls of the Alhambra are of little or no interest except as fields for decoration.

Two explanations can be given for this phenomenon. It may have derived from the poverty of the material used for construction. In the Alhambra there is no beautiful stone masonry such as is found in contemporary or earlier monuments in the Gothic West or in Egypt and Syria. Moreover, the western Islamic world never developed a technique of brickwork comparable to that of Iran. The hastily and cheaply assembled masonry in mortar and the friable bricks of fourteenth-century Granada had to be covered with some other material and did not lend themselves to any sort of complicated articulation. At the same time we need not assume that the fourteenth-century patrons had no sturdier material available to them, since Charles V and other Christian patrons of later times had access to excellent stone. It is therefore possible that the material of the Alhambra's walls was chosen consciously. If so, the choice reflected a major, although not exclusive, Islamic architectural practice. Many monuments, especially palaces, were built rapidly, either because insecurity of power made lengthy building programmes unlikely to reach a conclusion or because they tended to be personal rather than dynastic and were not meant or expected to survive their original patron. It is not necessary to attribute any profound philosophical and religious meanings to this tendency for cheaply built and heavily decorated walls, as has been done occasionally; the wall construction of the Alhambra may simply reflect a common medieval palace tradition.

Next to walls, the most characteristic means of support is marble columns. In line with a tradition which began with the mosque of Cordova in the eighth century, columns are short and

97. *The Court of the Lions, columns*

thin and are provided at their upper end with a variable number of ring-like mouldings [97]. Capitals, of standard shape, are divided into two zones: the lower one, of the same section as the column shaft, is usually decorated with a low-relief fret or band, while the upper part, which widens considerably, is provided with a heavy foliated decoration [98]. This development is characteristic of western Islamic architecture[9] and it is only occasionally that one encounters in the Alhambra the unified muqarnas capitals more typical of the eastern Mediterranean in the later Middle Ages [99]. Since columns were by tradition quite short and thin, the only means of raising their height and widening their base of support was to develop an elaborate system of imposts and impost blocks. The dimensions of the latter varied from place to

98. *The Court of the Lions, capital*

99. *The Cuarto Dorado, capital from the north side*

place, and in most instances their decoration serves to emphasize the vertical lines of the monumental unit in which they occur. Concern with imposts may have already begun in pre-Islamic Syrian architecture, but it became particularly marked in early Islamic times, when rapid construction of many new buildings with borrowed columns and capitals required the development of means to bring elements of different origins to the same level.

The column, the capital, and the impost are all forms of elevation developed by Islamic art from the heritage of classical art. The same origin identifies the superb carved wooden cornices, brackets, and modillions found in the eaves of the Cuarto Dorado and the Partal. A more typically Islamic feature is the wooden latticework found in windows. Most of the present examples are of modern workmanship, but there is no doubt that the original windows were provided with latticed woodwork in ways well illustrated in Egypt and Morocco.

Several means of spanning spaces are found in the Alhambra. In the external towers, the Alcazaba, and the major gateways, we encounter a wide range of domes on squinches [100] and of barrel or cross vaults. Even the later Tower of the Infantas contains a structurally interesting development of the cross vault into three polyhedra fitted into each other [101] and distinguishable only by the lines of their masonry. The architects of the Alhambra were clearly aware of a fairly wide range of technical developments of domes and vaults, but they chose not to use them directly in most of the elaborate parts of the palaces. It is only in the bath that we find simple horseshoe arches and domes on squinches or simple barrel vaults pierced with star-shaped openings for the escape of steam [102]. As in so much Islamic architecture before the fourteenth century, some of the most interesting technical developments occur in monuments of very practical use like fortresses or baths rather than in more formal ones. In Islamic as in many other architectural traditions, at least until very recent times, technical innovation was not particularly prized as a setting for private life

172

100. *The Gate of Arms, dome*

101. *The Tower of the Infantas, vault*

102. *The bath, dome*

and was restricted to places where its practical values could not be challenged.

In the formal parts of the Alhambra actual construction was generally not visible beneath the shell or sheath of wood or stucco. Both media were used for cupolas and vaults, and since they are the surfaces which were meant to be seen, it is with them that we must concern ourselves as we try to understand the building's architectural forms.

One can be fairly brief about wood, for, leaving aside the symbolic significance of the motifs, which were discussed earlier, or of the patterns of the designs, which will be mentioned later, the technique itself is clear enough. Known today as *artesonado*, it is a technique of wood mosaics in which small units of varying shapes, sizes, and sometimes colour are imbricated with each other or inlaid into each other. By the time of the Alhambra, it was already a well-developed technique, particularly well-known in Egypt and North Africa.[10] It was apparently first applied to objects, as we know from mihrabs, minbars, Koran stands, doors and small caskets from Egypt and elsewhere as early as in the eleventh century. It is not entirely excluded that there were also early architectural examples which have disappeared, but it is a technique which, in its working up of details, is remarkably suited to small objects. The point has some importance for our understanding of the Alhambra's aesthetic values, which lies in its implication of the architectural monument as a sort of object, that is, a work of art in which surface values and concentration of attention on progressively smaller features predominate over masses and the interplay of volumes.

Stucco played a far more important part in the creation of the Alhambra's inner elevation. Arches between columns, segments of vaults or wide arches between narrow walls, ceilings over many rectangular spaces as well as cupolas, in fact almost all the means to cover an open area appear through a sheath of stucco. Except for a few arches, their composition is based on the muqarnas, frequently called stalactite or honeycomb. Since it is a unique Islamic form, and since it is almost impossible to understand the Alhambra without understanding its purpose and range of possibilities, we must try to define the muqarnas and describe its properties as precisely as possible.[11] The difficulty is that its origins and its historic development are unfortunately still very unclear.

So far as is known, the origins of the muqarnas probably lie in almost simultaneous but apparently unconnected developments in north-eastern Iran and central North Africa. In Iran, the Metropolitan Museum excavations at Nishapur brought to light a group of small curved stucco units, whose inner concave side only was decorated with paintings. It has been proposed, without definite proof but as a likely hypothesis, that these units were meant to be assembled into combinations and then placed on walls, providing the latter with a highly articulated three-dimensional surface. The Nishapur finds are probably earlier than the middle of the tenth century. Then in the mausoleum of Tim, near Bukhara in Soviet Central Asia, which can be dated to *c.* 976, the very same curved shapes are assembled in brick in the

103. Ardistan, mosque, vaults

squinches of the octagon below the dome. This is the earliest dated instance of the realization that the curved shape of the Nishapur fragments could be assimilated to a segment of vault and that various combinations of such shapes could be used both architectonically and decoratively, as they were to be in full magnificence in the mosques of western Iran in the second half of the eleventh century [103].[12]

The evidence from North Africa is of the eleventh century, somewhat later than its Iranian counterpart. In the Qal'ah of the Beni Hammad large numbers of plaster fragments and curiously shaped ceramics were found. The former were probably parts of a stucco niche consisting of segments of vaults comparable to the Iranian examples, and the latter probably formed a cluster of polyhedral ceramic units fitted together as a mass.[13] These formed a large composition projecting from the ceiling; their external surface was as complicated as on the first group but without its emphasis on concave curves [104].

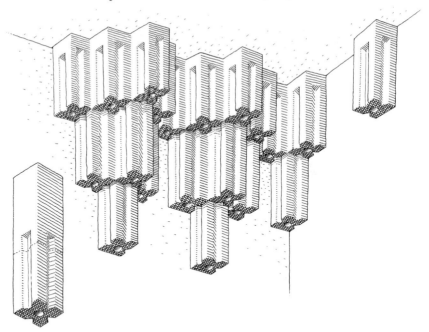

104. *The Qal'ah of the Beni Hammad, muqarnas*

Whether or not the two developments in Iran and North Africa are related, two points about these new forms are of importance. One is that, from the late eleventh century on, all Muslim lands adopted and developed the muqarnas, which became almost as common a feature of an elevation as the Corinthian capital in antiquity. The second and far more important point is that, from the moment of its first appearance, the muqarnas acquired four characteristic attributes, whose evolution and characteristics form its history: it was three-dimensional and therefore provided volume wherever it was used, the nature and depth of the volume being left to the discretion of the maker; it could be used both as an architectonic form, because of its relationship to vaults, and as an applied ornament, because its depth could be controlled; it had no intrinsic limits, since not one of its elements is a finite unit of composition and there is no logical or mathematical limitation to the scale of any one composition; and it was a volume which could be a solid or a void, a projecting mass of complex shapes or a complex outline – a three-dimensional unit which could be resolved into a two-dimensional outline.

It is not relevant to our present purpose to speculate why the whole Muslim world adopted the muqarnas with such ease and alacrity, or whether ornamental or structural considerations predominated in its formation. What is important is that the Alhambra is one of the very few monuments in existence which utilized practically all the muqarnas's characteristics. The analysis of the muqarnas made by Goury and Jones[14] indicated that only seven different prisms are involved in most constructions

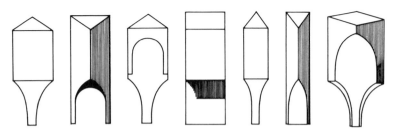

105. Muqarnas, details

178

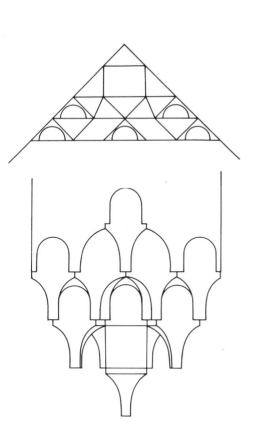

106. Muqarnas, details

107. The Hall of the Two Sisters,
analysis of the dome

[105 and 106], and some five thousand of them were used in the dome of the Hall of the Two Sisters [107]. There are only three sections to the prisms: right-angled triangle, rectangle, and isosceles triangle. What makes variety of composition possible is that there are several facets on each prism and that these facets are at different angles from each other and have different curvatures. But at least one of the surfaces is common to more than one unit, so that a large number of different arrangements can be made with a small number of units.

The muqarnas was used in large domes, as in the two halls of the complex of the Lions [50 and 53], in smaller domes [43], in niches [25 and 26], on arches [108], and as an almost flat decora-

108. *The Court of the Lions, detail of colonnade*

tive frieze [20]. In each instance the module as well as the depth of the composition was different and adapted to the size of the area involved or to the required purpose. In ceilings it served a clear architectonic aim, or at the very least provided the structural illusion of an ascending movement culminating in a small cupola.

Thanks to the flexibility of its small units, it could be adapted to any kind of polygon and succeeded in giving a domical effect to rectangular spaces. But it was also occasionally almost flat, and in the small alcoves of the Hall of the Ambassadors it becomes no more than a small festoon. In all instances, its effect was entirely controlled: in the large cupolas it serves as a sort of expensive tent hung over space; in the arcades of the Hall of the Kings [44 and 45] or in the zones of transition of the great domes, a sense of overhanging masses tends to predominate. There is in fact, as so often in the better monuments of Islamic art, a certain ambivalence about the meaning to be given to the forms. The choice of interpretation or of emphasis lies for the most part with the viewer, who can decide to focus his attention on the motif in many different ways. Nowhere does this ambivalence appear more clearly than in the Hall of the Kings, where the muqarnas serves as means to span an open space, as the main rhythm of the composition, and as a delicately complex profile of an archway, either a lace-like border or carefully balanced hangings from the ceiling. Yet in almost all instances it is structurally nothing more than a sheath of stucco over a mosaic brick vault.

However, if the muqarnas was employed in the Alhambra with a full knowledge of its versatility and its potential, it was not used in any new or original way. By the twelfth century in monuments of Marrakesh and Fez,[15] not to mention Egyptian ones of the twelfth century or Iranian ones from the twelfth century on, Muslim artisans were to develop in a truly sophisticated manner the architectonic possibilities of the muqarnas and also its potential as a cheap replacement for complicated ceiling masonries. The latter aspect is at times present in the Alhambra, but the more interesting and historically significant side to its muqarnas is that, even though complex and sophisticated in its versatility, it is almost never innovative. The contrast with fourteenth-century architecture in Anatolia, Iran and, to a slightly smaller degree, Egypt and Syria is very striking and well illustrates a point to which we shall return in conclusion, that the Alhambra stands at the end of a historical development and is, despite all its perfection, a formal dead end.

Walls, columns, wooden and muqarnas ceilings constitute the main elements of the Alhambra's elevation, the basic terms of its visible structure. But these terms were not set up arbitrarily or as simple responses to functional or symbolic purposes. In attempting to discuss the syntax of the Alhambra's elevation, we are on far less secure grounds than in dealing with the morphology, partly because of the lack of precise metrological studies and partly because very little thought has been given to the problems and procedures of such analyses in Islamic architecture. Their potential has been demonstrated by Georges Marçais in a brilliant analysis of the organization of the Court of the Lions.[16] Starting with the generally accepted observation that the Court and its portico seem to be far more open and airier than they are in reality, with their small size and large number of columns and arches, he noted that the apparent symmetry of the Court along two main axes was not followed in such details as the location of single or double columns and of high rounded arches or lower ones with a muqarnas profile. A detailed analysis of the northeastern corner of the Court [109] showed that, in this quarter alone, there are five separate axes of composition which overlap each other in such a fashion that any one bay may belong to more than one unit of composition. Furthermore, arches and columns serve two separate functions: to relate symmetrical units to each other and to recall or echo each other. Finally, the succession of symmetrical units is based only partly on the composition of the plan, for it is the flattening out of the portico into a two-dimensional scheme which reveals the complexity of its arrangement. In this respect, the compositional order of the monument is strikingly similar to a muqarnas, for it is at the same time a linear system and an organization of masses. If we add to Marçais's observations the fact that the proportions between parts in the elevation of the portico are organized according to the irrational principles of the Golden Mean, we can justifiably con-

182

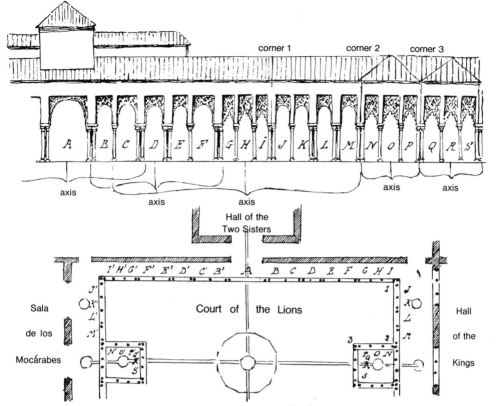

109. *The Court of the Lions, analysis of the north-eastern quarter*

clude that the Court of the Lions was an extraordinarily carefully thought-out composition, even more striking in its elevation than in its plan.

It is far more difficult to assess its originality. As Marçais pointed out, already in the ninth century the compositional principle of overlapping axes was exhibited in the arcaded façade in Kairouan's congregational mosque, and the Moroccan *madrasahs* of the fourteenth century used the same principles as the Alhambra's in the decorative organization of their interior courts. As to the Golden Mean, and its simpler version of alternating rational and irrational ratios as in progressive squares, they are present in Central Asia and in eleventh-century Isfahan. As in so many instances already discussed, the originality of the

Alhambra lies less in the presence or invention of any one theme than in the simultaneous existence of so many.

But, beyond the question of the sources of the compositional pattern of the Court of the Lions, the broader issues are whether the complexity of the Court's arrangement can be extended to the rest of the Alhambra and what the point of these devices may have been. In the absence of detailed studies, an answer to the first question can only be suggested. It is likely that an analysis of the Halls of the Two Sisters and of the Abencerrajes will bring out a similarly complex elevation. But the Court of the Myrtles and the Hall of the Ambassadors do not seem to exhibit the same concerns. The former [21 and 22] is much more of an additive composition in which a very simple balancing of masses around a single vertical axis dominates. In fact, its arrangement of two towers framing a portico in front of a central high and massive tower harks back in a strikingly archaic fashion to the very ancient Oriental type of the *beit hilani* which exercised so many scholars half a century ago.[17] The Hall of the Ambassadors is also much simpler than its counterparts to the east, and its surface ornament takes precedence over its architectonic composition. The same conclusion seems to be appropriate for the Cuarto Dorado.

As to the point of the devices employed in the Court of the Lions, two considerations deserve mention. One is that complexity of composition and especially the superimposition of different orders of organization in elevation serve to increase the monument's size. This increase is accomplished not so much by a system of *trompe-l'œil* effects like those developed in late Renaissance and Baroque art as by multiplying the number and nature of the visual impressions produced by the monument. Space is suggested by the multitude of different visual planes and points of view, as though there were no end to the monument's directions.

The other and related consideration is the almost infinite division of any perceptible or identifiable part into smaller units. The Court of the Lions does not lead outward but inward, because its composition and each of the composition's constituent parts force the observer into the consideration of ever smaller details. It is not, however, a single ensemble which subdivides itself into logical parts, as in a classical Gothic cathedral for instance, but several superimposed schemes, each with a logic of its own.

The overwhelming objective of the Alhambra's elevation lies in its seeking to provide what may be called illusions, that is, impressions and effects which are different from the architectural or decorative means used to create them. From the very rough contrast between its external and internal profiles all the way to the analysis of a single bay in the Court of Lions or the muqarnas, we may discover a consistent attempt to give the impression that things are not quite what they seem to be. These impressions are heightened by any number of other syntactic devices, for instance the peculiar rhythm of the sources of light in the ensemble of the Lions. A north–south section [41] shows a central source in the court itself, then areas of chiaroscuro and darkness until secondary sources provided by the base of the main domes and by the Mirador de la Daraxa introduce more subdued beams into the building. But it is not simply a question of contrasts during daylight; the monument is so composed that at night, when light comes from covered halls and darkness reigns outside, it becomes visible and perceptible as an exact negative of its positive reality during the day. Aesthetically this coexistence of two opposite but equal perceptions is a strikingly contemporary phenomenon, visible in many skyscrapers. But in the Alhambra its purpose was less to glorify materials and construction than to provide the viewer or the user with constant surprises and the illusion of a rich setting in a simple medium. As I sought to show in the previous chapter, this illusion has at times an iconographic meaning, but the more important point at this stage is that it reflects a concern which typifies Iranian architecture as well, from the fourteenth century onward, and possibly also Iranian miniatures. In the latter handsomely dressed princes and attendants sit and play in or around magnificent buildings or gardens, with-

110. Humay and Humayun in a garden, illustrating Khvaju Kirmani's poem
Humay and Humayun *in a Persian manuscript dated 1396*

111. Humay at the gate of Humayun's castle, from the same manuscript

out any clear indication whether they are being shown at night or by day [110 and 111]. Or, if an indication exists, it hardly affects the nature or mood of the activities, which are in reality outside time and space. The Alhambra is an architectural translation of this very same mood, although its specific forms are Spanish and North African and not Iranian.

SURFACE DECORATION

Surface decoration is the most obvious and most frequently mentioned feature of the Alhambra, but, curiously enough, it has never been discussed in any systematic manner. Part of the reason is that, since there is no generally accepted vocabulary for Islamic decoration, the alternative of long descriptions and dull arguments about appropriateness of terms has, perhaps mercifully, been avoided. Another reason is that there is no published record of scaled drawings and photographs. As a result we only have partial lists of motifs,[18] several broader considerations of geometry in ornament, including a doctoral dissertation in mathematics, which is not easily accessible to non-mathematicians,[19] and a few very general considerations of ornament.[20] No doubt the decoration of the walls of the Alhambra will be fully understood only when it is subjected to systematic analyses of thematic and stylistic details like those initiated by M. Dimand for early Islamic art[21] or to studies of principles of organization and methods of actual work like those of Rempel for Central Asia.[22] In the absence of these investigations, I shall limit myself to a few considerations of two main topics: the uses and techniques of the decoration and the formal meanings which can be attributed to it.

The lower parts of almost all walls are covered with mosaic tiles – generally white, red, yellow, blue, and green – and the rest with stucco; wood occurs almost exclusively in ceilings or in strictly architectural units like beams or eaves. Both wooded fragments and stucco are painted. For the colours of the latter, authenticity cannot always be guaranteed, but for the former the inscriptions discovered in the Hall of the Ambassadors should provide important information about the colour programmes in the monument as a whole. Tiles, stucco, and wood are not particularly original techniques and even the vertical sequence, from tiles to wood, in which they are used at the Alhambra is characteristic of much of western Islamic architecture. The only question, so far unanswered, is why this particular region of Islamic art limited its use of coloured tiles to the lower parts of walls (with a few exceptions only, as in the Puerta del Vino) and did not develop the complex subject-matter found on tiles in Iran or in Anatolia. Part of the answer lies in the fact that decoration in palaces tended to be less permanent, possibly because it was expected to be frequently modified. The Alhambra Museum has preserved several fragments of stucco which bear on the back imprints of an earlier and different design, thus indicating that changes occurred. But, even though the secular and private character of the Alhambra may explain the limitations of the use of tiles in this one monument, some deeper cause must have affected the rest of western Islamic architectural decoration.

A related question is that of the formal organization of decoration. It has been argued that all compositions within any one room begin with some major ensemble, the mihrab in an oratory [17], gates or windows in other halls [20, 31, 49 and 52]. It is indeed true that every opening, even bays in the Court of the Lions, tends to form an independent unit of ornamentation, with a rectangular narrow frame and a variety of devices filling spandrels. It is also true that, in the Hall of the Ambassadors for instance, the points of separation between different arrangements of ornament are determined by the height and location of doors and windows. Yet it does not seem entirely justified to conclude that what Marçais called 'les grands ensembles' served either as the modular units of the decoration or as its main axis. In each hall, instead, decorations sought to determine as large a quadrangular surface as was possible and then to use each such surface as a single unit. The result is that narrow vertical panels around an opening alternate occasionally with huge horizontal ones, as in the Hall of the Ambassadors, but the basic unit of composition throughout is the rectangular panel, regardless of its association with an opening. It is likely that one reason for this predilection was the nature of the geometry used in the designs, to which we shall return presently. But it is intriguing to note that

112. *Isfahan, Lutfallah's mosque*

the same tendency to rectangular units of composition occurs
also in Iran, for instance in most of the great Safavid monuments
of Isfahan [112], and it is possible that, beyond the requirements
of designs, there remained in the background of the Alhambra
decoration the memory of textiles and of rugs hung on walls. The

possibility is strengthened when we recall that one of the most spectacular monuments of architectonic ceramics from Muslim Spain, the so-called Fortuny panel from the early fifteenth century [113], is an obvious imitation of a rug.[23]

113.
The Fortuny panel

While large panels defined by available architectural surfaces and functional fixtures like doors and bays form the main units of surface decoration, they are not the only ones. For one of the fascinating aspects of the Alhambra and yet another illustration of the characteristic inward movement of its art is that almost every facet of a muqarnas composition was provided with an ornament in the same techniques and with similar designs to the ones used in large ensembles. Although architecture and construction imposed certain hierarchies of size and dimension, there was apparently no hierarchy in the quality and nature of decoration. Every available surface was ornamented, or at least could be. The result is a contradiction. On the one hand it is as though the whole monument acquired a veneer, like the glaze over a ceramic or the polish of woodwork. But, at the same time, if every part of the monument is ornamented equally in quality and quantity, does this not mean that no particular meaning or significance should be attributed to any single design or motif?

This question is not peculiar to the Alhambra; it is in fact the central question of Muslim ornament, at least after the magnificent arbitrariness of Mshatta's façade in the middle of the eighth century.[24] In order to suggest an answer, we must look at the Alhambra's decoration from the point of view of the possible meanings of its forms. There are only three basic motifs. The first is writing, used exclusively in small cartouches or long bands, and, as we have already shown, writing is a concrete iconographic sign in the building. The second is vegetal, consisting of derivatives from the pine cone, the acanthus, and the palmette;[25] it is on the whole a very impoverished and limited vocabulary, and I know of no instance where some detail of composition or some deviation from repetitive norm might suggest, even faintly, the likelihood of any deeper significance than that of simply covering a surface. This is all the more curious since earlier examples of vegetal motifs do indicate the possibility of special formal, if not always iconographic, meanings,[26] and since gardens and plants played such an important role in the Alhambra.

The third motif is geometry, which appears both by itself, as in most of the tiled panels, and as the governing principle of most designs with vegetal elements. In both instances the main objective of the ornament was to cover the whole surface of a panel. As can be seen on several tile fragments [114 and 115], there is no design set on a background, as occurs for instance in classical ornament; every single space is an active participant in the

114. *The Court of the Myrtles, tile decoration*

115. *The Mirador de la Daraxa, tile decoration*

ornamentation. It is less a case of *horror vacui*, as it has so frequently been defined, than a much more positive attempt at making every part of the surface significant. The key geometric principles involved appear to be the following: symmetry, which permits easy repetition in a composition; a single unit of composition (usually a square or a polygon) which is small enough to be unobtrusive and simple enough to lend itself to a large variety of modifications; linear growth, whereby any one closed geometric unit such as a square or a circle can be transformed or replaced by straight or broken lines of infinite growth; rotation along two or more axes, which provides the major directions of ornament. Each one of these principles – and there are others, no doubt – has its own set of abstract properties and, as has been demonstrated for symmetry,[27] there is a large but finite number of mathematical possibilities for each of them. Geometric principles were applied to floral ornament as well, either through the creation of a grid of interlace – usually based on a star-shaped polygon – separating vegetal motifs or through geometrization of vegetal forms [35 and 116].

116. *The Hall of the Ambassadors,*
detail of ornament showing geometrization of vegetal form

The overwhelming presence of geometry in the surface ornamentation of the Alhambra has, from Owen Jones and Girault de Prangey to J. Bronowski in his BBC talks,[28] been recognized as a profoundly Islamic phenomenon reflecting certain universal characteristics and values. And several recent investigations in Iran and Central Asia have posed in a new fashion the various issues of the relationship between mathematics and ornament in Islamic art.[29] Two of these issues are of importance to our purpose in explaining the Alhambra.

The first is essentially historical. In so far as it can be imagined from rather meagre sources, it was in the tenth century, most probably in the ecumenical capital of Baghdad and in Iran, that a conjunction of cultural forces (the availability of Greek and Hindu scientific thought, the so-called Iranian Renaissance) and social ones (the broadening of the ethnic, intellectual, and economic patronage of the arts and belles-lettres) modified the direction taken from the very beginning of Islamic art by a decoration from which living beings were absent, or at the very least rare.[30] Characteristic geometric designs of earlier times, as in Umayyad palaces or in a Samanid house in Samarqand,[31] consisted primarily of additive combinations of simple geometric forms such as squares, circles, or diamonds, sometimes with original systems of proportions (investigated by Rempel) but more often used as simple frames around other types of motifs, mostly floral. Almost always the dimensions and extent of the ornament were determined by the area available on the architectural monument or the object. After the tenth century a second type of ornament appears alongside the earlier one. Emphasizing polygons and stars, it makes geometric pattern almost the only subject of decoration; it penetrates into the very fabric of wall construction, as in eleventh- and twelfth-century mausoleums and minarets in Iran; it subdivides small units into small parts and rotates them in a variety of ways; and it becomes an end in itself more readily defined through its subsumed mathematical structure than through its visible combination of motifs. From evidence which is only now being discovered,[32] it seems that this new manner was made possible by a conscious attempt on the part of professional mathematicians and scientists to explain and to guide the work of artisans.

Whatever the explanation of this tenth-century phenomenon may be, it became an integral part of Islamic culture and spread westward. In the conservative world of Morocco or Spain its abstract values were carefully preserved and nurtured, and it should be recalled that, at least in the eleventh century, Toledo was a major centre of scientific learning. But by the fourteenth century mathematical creativity was no longer a characteristic of western Islam, and some doubt may be raised whether the Alhambra's varieties of geometric combinations derive from a conscious knowledge of mathematical properties rather than from a long history of artisanal work. For, especially when compared to Iranian developments since the tenth century, the ornament of the Alhambra is lacking in warmth and inventiveness, despite its technical virtuosity.

The limitations I am suggesting for this decoration as a historical document need not affect its formal and possibly symbolic importance. For, beyond the strictly visual observations made earlier, the fascination of the Alhambra designers, especially in tile-work, for ambiguous effects involving the totality of the surface to be decorated has struck many observers as far more profound than mere technical virtuosity. It is interesting to note that Maurits Escher made many drawings from the Alhambra in the course of his own exciting experiments in visual perception. A recent student of Escher, and Professor Bronowski, have pointed out that all such experiments find their parallel in the fundamental principles of the transformations of crystals and their mathematical formulation.[33] The implication is that the type of ornament used in the Alhambra satisfies and excites precisely because its mathematical definition is the same as that which, since Pythagoras, has been used to explain most physical phenomena, from music to the stars. And, while it is a formulation which failed to explain motion, it is applicable to the inner structure of unchanging matter, such as crystals. If we recall our argument in the previous chapter that the main halls around the Court of the Lions were wilfully endowed with cosmic significance, it may be possible to argue further that this significance was carried down to the smallest detail of ornament and that each one of these details reflected an aspect, a 'transformation', of mathematical formulas depicting the universe. This conclusion would find a parallel in a number of the contemporary and later Iranian developments of ornament which have been recently explained in like fashion as visual translations of the cosmic view of Islamic mysticism.[34]

All of this is possible and it requires further and more systematic refinement. Yet, without denying a built-in Islamic mode of representation which automatically sought abstract formulas for whatever it wanted to express, I have some doubt about the degree of consciousness which can be assumed for the sum of the Alhambra's decorative designs; it seems to me preferable to conclude that by the fourteenth century these designs were formal redundancies whose deeper meaning can be demonstrated only at a much earlier time.

One last point about the meaning of the ornament in the Alhambra concerns possible distinctions of values within the various motifs. The lack of any hierarchy of decorated areas, combined with the repetitiveness of motifs, makes one wonder whether some other variant was significant. The most important variant may be called the density of the design, that is, the complexity and elaborateness of the treatment of the surface. It is differences in density which distinguish the central alcove of the Hall of the Ambassadors [34] from the side ones [31], and the Hall of the Two Sisters [49] from the Hall of the Kings [44]. To the extent that variations in density appear to correspond to major architectural concerns, it seems proper to conclude that attempts were made to develop a very subdued hierarchy in the intensity of decoration which is perceptible only after detailed analyses of very similar motifs. In most instances it is the internal complexity of the geometric gridwork rather than any one specific motif which determined this hierarchy.

Although the main techniques of surface decoration consisted of tiles and of stucco, a word must be said about mural paintings. In the Partal, very badly damaged early fourteenth-century friezes of personages in all sorts of activities (mostly drinking, hunting, travelling) appear to illustrate a very typical Muslim concern with princely life as an expression of well-being and pleasure.[35] Then the three strange ceiling paintings in the Hall of the Kings [46–8] may have had the same significance, but there is still some doubt about their date and a great deal of uncertainty about their subject-matter.[36]

Although it may be impossible, in our present state of knowledge, to suggest any conclusions or specific answers to the questions with which we began, we can perhaps make a number of observations which may serve as working hypotheses. One such point is that the Alhambra, or rather any one of its constituent parts, almost always resembles an artefact rather than a building. From whatever point of view its forms are discussed, analysis tends to focus on textures which are meant to be contemplated singly, in depth, and which break down into an infinite number of small parts, whereas any one of the parts does not necessarily lead back to the complete architectural monument. This tendency to see a monument of architecture as a precious object is one of the most consistent features of Islamic art, especially in its more private works such as palace pavilions or mausoleums. But it is probably not entirely correct to understand the Alhambra simply as a magnification into construction of an object for private use. It is rather that in one of its manifold aspects, perhaps the most uniquely original one, Islamic art enjoyed mixing forms. In a celebrated bronze lamp in Fez, a work of metal appears like a cupola with typically architectonic ribs.[37] The error of appreciation lies in seeking within Islamic art the classical distinction between arts with fully developed aesthetic aims and techniques with practical ones.

A second point about the forms of the Alhambra is that they are neither numerous nor particularly original. Their vocabulary belongs almost entirely to the decorative language developed in Morocco and Spain during the twelfth and thirteenth centuries, the so-called Almoravid and Almohad periods. But their composition and frequently their origins relate many of them to the Near East, either the eighth and ninth centuries in Syria and Iraq, or Iran from the tenth century onward. But, whatever their origins and however typical they may be of a given sub-culture, their arrangement in the Alhambra and their quality are unique. Arrangement and quality occur at two levels. One is that of technical competence, and I have tried to show that, especially in the elevation of the Court of the Lions and in the geometry of surface decoration, elaborate and complex planning was involved. But the other level is perhaps more important, since it better defines the character or mood of the monument. In part it is a secretive level, in that exteriors do not reflect interiors; open and covered spaces are wilfully confused; designs of all sorts lead one away from the ensemble into a most minute muqarnas facet or a single leafy motif; negative and positive, or solid and void, are deliberately confused. One is rarely led to a focal point; one has to be in the midst of it to realize it. This secretiveness is in fact a creation of illusions and ambiguities, almost as in a theatrical performance. The terms of the illusion are obviously bound to Islamic culture and even more specifically to its western sub-culture. But the notion of a palace as a mythopoetic source of illusions is not peculiar to Islam. From the hanging gardens of Babylon to Nero's palaces in Rome with their *trompe-l'œil* ceilings, to the Byzantine palaces of Constantinople with their roaring lions, singing trees, and emperors descending from the heavens, and even to the Versailles of the *Roi-Soleil*, the royal setting was meant to suggest the illusion of another and better life. For, to modify slightly a perceptive remark of John Summerson, the

117. *Marrakesh, Sa'di mausoleums*

whole of the Alhambra is but an assemblage of 'heavenly mansions',[38] which, almost by definition, can never be anything but
illusions on earth.

One last point about the forms of the Alhambra is perhaps
more negative. There is very little innovation or inventiveness in

118. *Fez, Qarawin mosque, courtyard and pavilion*

it. And it is striking that works of *mudejar* art, like the Alcazar of Seville, or later masterpieces of Moroccan architecture, like the Sa'di mausoleums in Marrakesh [117][39] and the sixteenth-century pavilion, almost directly copied from the Alhambra, in the Qarawin mosque [118] and the Madrasah Bouanania [119] in Fez,[40] picked up the external themes, mostly surface decoration, of the Alhambra but failed for the most part to renew them or to integrate them into original architectural forms. For, whereas Turkish Anatolia, Mongol Iran, and to a smaller degree Mamluk Egypt were all able in the fourteenth century to invent new architectural and decorative forms and to initiate changes (sometimes revolutionary ones) in construction and in planning, Muslim Spain simply summed up in unique and almost perfect fashion several centuries of formal developments.

119. Fez, Madrasah Bouanania

CONCLUSION:
THE ALHAMBRA,
A REVERIE
OF THE PAST

The peculiar charm of this old dreamy palace is its power of calling up vague reveries and picturings of the past, and thus clothing naked realities with the illusions of the memory and the imagination.

Washington Irving, *The Alhambra*[1]

The main historical question raised at the beginning of this book was whether the Alhambra is a fortunately but accidentally preserved example of a fairly widespread tradition of princely buildings or whether it is indeed the unique monument it appears to be. A second question derived from the functional as well as the aesthetic characteristics of the building: what are the nature and causes of its striking impact on visitors, from Romantic literati to present-day tourists. An unusual range of individual tastes and interests, since Ferdinand and Isabella, have found in the Alhambra solace, pleasure, inspiration, and that sensuous and poetic 'reverie of the past' which so enchanted Washington Irving.

The preceding pages sought to provide some of the elements with which to answer these questions and to explain the monument's magnetism. We were led in many different directions, from the medieval mythology of Solomon the King-Prophet to the intricacies of the muqarnas and the interpretation of ornament. That it should be so is, first of all, a demonstration of the monument's importance as a conscious work of art, for almost every one of its identifiable characteristics leads to the consideration of questions and of monuments which are remote from the Alhambra in time and in space. Neither has been exhausted, sometimes for lack of sufficient information, sometimes because their elaboration and interpretation would have led us too far afield. Among particularly noteworthy instances are such topics as systems of proportion in planning, elevation, and decoration, which require measurements so far unavailable; the history and character of gardens and in general of vegetation and architecture, which demand complex textual investigations; the development and background of individual decorative motifs, which cannot be achieved without monographic studies of details; and the daily and ceremonial lives of princes, for which literary sources are essential. And there may be others, for, like any masterpiece, the Alhambra is relevant to almost any question about man's aesthetic creativity, its causes and its effects.

Within the limits of the historical, iconographic, and formal discussions which have been pursued, however, three kinds of conclusions emerge. The first is local and limited to western Islam in the fourteenth century. Situated between a bustling town in the valley and semi-private gardens above, a typical feudal city was developed in the thirteenth century; this city was transformed by the building of a stunning architectural composition, the complex of the Lions, by the decoration of previously existing halls and courts, and by the addition of unusual monuments like the Puerta del Vino. A setting of dwellings, gardens, and pavilions which apparently, until that time, was hardly atypical or unusually distinguished was utterly modified by the striking quality of this accomplishment and by the ideological self-consciousness of its literary commentary. I have attributed this modification to Muhammad V and proposed that he sought to commemorate at the same time his return to the throne (1362) and his victory over the Christians at Algeciras (1369). It is possible that he sought inspiration from the memory and remains of the palace erected in the eleventh century by the Jewish viziers of Granada, but it seems more likely that the ideas which find expression in the Alhambra belong to a generalized mood of medieval Islam and of the Middle Ages as a whole. We shall return to the nature of the mood presently as well as to the Alhambra's functions and purposes, which are more significant in a wide context than in a limited western Islamic one. This is much less so for the architectural elements and composition, since almost all of them, from the slender columns and two-tiered capitals to the elaborate muqarnas or to the combination of courts and long or square halls, belong to the idiom developed from the twelfth century onwards in Morocco and Spain. Even though some have their origins or close parallels in the Muslim Near East, there is no evidence of formal influences from the east in the fourteenth century, and the impact of the Alhambra and the styles it reflects is limited to *mudejar* art in Spain and to Morocco. It is striking to observe that neither in architectural planning and construction nor in decoration did the Alhambra truly innovate. Thirteenth-century *mudejar* art in Toledo, the art of Seville until the fifteenth century, and Moroccan monuments as late as the seventeenth century in Marrakesh, all use the language of the Alhambra, with only minor variations in quality.[2] This conservatism was no doubt a reflection of the social and especially the intellectual and cultural atmosphere of North African and Spanish Islam in the later Middle Ages. The contrast with Egypt and even more so with Iran and Anatolia is quite striking.

The positive side of this conservatism lies in the elaborate classicism of its forms. Even if at times repetitive and obvious, the forms of the Alhambra are perfect in the sense that each of them is developed and used with a full awareness of its possibilities and with visual clarity and logic in spite of their complexity. The same clarity and logic are not always present in the later buildings of Morocco or in some *mudejar* ones. At the local level of western Islamic art of the late Middle Ages, the transformation of the Alhambra under Muhammad V appears as the perfect expression of a unique regional tradition. Even though inspired by a comparatively minor dynastic and military occurrence, it crystallized the possibilities as well as the limits of that tradition.

But the importance of the Alhambra does not lie only at this local level. I have sought, with several examples, to demonstrate that the Alhambra reflected a complex princely tradition. The manner in which this tradition is made visible is very original, since forms of local origin were given meaning by the addition to them of the iconography of the written word. Thus the Hall of the Ambassadors and the south hall of the Court of the Lions or the Hall of the Two Sisters and the Hall of the Kings share the same decoration, techniques, and ceiling types. But inscriptions in the Halls of the Ambassadors and of the Two Sisters endowed these rooms with cosmic significance. The Fountain of the Lions is perhaps more immediately significant iconographically, but even there it is a poem actually carved on it and another describing something like it which suggested the fountain's meaning. This method of signifying is a unique characteristic of Islamic art generally, since its first major building, the Dome of the Rock in Jerusalem;[3] unfortunately, its subsequent development has barely been investigated.[4] But the ideas which were expressed are of even greater interest than the method used. I have tried to show that the patron and the builders of the Alhambra attempted to reproduce rotating domes of heaven, paradisial settings, and other motifs belonging to an art of princes with pre-Islamic roots in classical antiquity and in the ancient Orient. Whatever their origins, most of the themes associated with this tradition seem to have coalesced around the person of Solomon. It is easy to see why the King-Prophet acquired so many attributes in the Muslim tradition, for already in the Koran he appears as the master of the wonderful and of the unique, for whom the jinns 'fashion whatever he wanted: halls, statues, bowls like water-troughs, and pots' (XXXIV, 12–13). We are not likely ever to unravel the specific mechanisms by which Solomonic associations began, although some recent work has outlined what happened in the Solomonic mythology around Persepolis in Iran.[5] Much of this development probably first occurred at a folk level, which is notoriously difficult to localize and to date adequately. A further and more important aspect of the Solomonic tradition is that it is not uniquely Islamic, for it appears in medieval Jewish and Christian sources as well, and it continued in Renaissance and later arts in the West.

In this iconographic respect the Alhambra belongs quite obviously to a much wider context than the local western Islamic one of the Middle Ages. Similarly its composition and functions also relate it to several Near Eastern Islamic and even earlier traditions. In fact, it appears almost as a sort of summary of most of the ways in which royal architecture developed since Khorsabad or, at the very least, the imperial palaces of Rome. That this is so, in spite of the dissimilarity of forms, can be explained by the structural permanence of princely art throughout the Middle Ages. Just as objects were interchangeable between Constantinople and Cairo, so were the aims of princely setting alike in the most divergent cultural settings.[6] There are probably several reasons for this phenomenon, which continued in many ways until the end of the First World War, but one of them is certainly that all medieval traditions were heirs to the same Hellenistic-Roman synthesis of artistic purposes and ideas of Mediterranean and Oriental regions,[7] even when forms differed immensely.

The interesting aspect of the Alhambra in this connection is that the significance of its forms and of its associations was no longer understood precisely at the time when western Renaissance architects and artists returned consciously to the classical models from which so many of the Alhambra's meanings and forms derived. This is so in part because fourteenth-century Spain did not understand the sources of its own ideas as classical, but regarded them as its own. The Alhambra does indeed illustrate an ideological revival, and it does possess something of the contrived and self-consciously elaborate aspect of a revival. But it is the revival of the Islamic synthesis of classical and ancient Near Eastern motifs which had taken place in Baghdad, Cordova, and Cairo many centuries earlier. It was there that all sorts of other themes, formal ones such as effects of surprise or the muqarnas as well as metaphors and images such as the comparisons of palaces with brides, came into being and were added to the more universal Solomonic mythology. The medieval and Islamic mood of *The Thousand and One Nights* obscured or rather modified the ancient and classical idea of domes of heaven, just as the passion for ornament has made almost unrecognizable the Roman and Hellenistic sources of the arches and columns of the Alhambra. By the time Mediterranean culture re-established its formal relationship to antiquity, the genetic mutations of antique forms and ideas found in the Alhambra could no longer be understood except as an alien exoticism.[8]

These conclusions about the meanings and associations of the Alhambra's forms belong to what may be called the ideological and typological levels of the Alhambra. But there is another level, that of the purely formal and aesthetic. Regardless of the meanings, associations, and functions which can clearly be seen in it or which were given to it at the time of its creation as well as in historical perspective, the Alhambra is a monument of intrinsic aesthetic value. The most significant conclusion to draw at this level is that, beyond the complexities of a single composition like that of the ensemble of the Court of the Lions, every part of the Alhambra exhibits two consistent features. The first is that every unit was an intentionally 'interiorized' creation to be seen, appreciated, and used from the inside. Relatively simple in the Generalife, the Partal, or the complex of the Myrtles, this interiorization was unusually elaborate in the Court of the Lions. As well as creating architectural compositions which are meaningful only from the inside, the artists of the Alhambra developed ornamental and architectural forms which subdivided themselves into almost infinitely smaller elements. They invited and still invite a unique search for the inner principle or the single unit which makes the whole possible.

The other feature is the sensuousness of the forms, whereby walls, columns, ceilings, water, at times space itself are not fixed constants and definite compositions but become almost alive with sinuous lines and profiles, with moving surfaces or ornament, and are endlessly affected by a changing and contrasting light. Only colour has been too much eroded to be effectively analysed, although it was certainly present, perhaps even garishly so, in the past.

Interiorization and sensuousness are not merely physical attributes of the Alhambra. They are the consequences of the fact that so few concrete functions can be given to any one of its parts. For these were not buildings which imposed certain activities on the men inside them. They were shells for whatever man did, and their character was supposed to be such that pleasure, exhilaration, and excitement were to be generated or heightened by the very fact that these activities took place in them. At this level, the Alhambra was indeed a beautiful object which could transfigure the daily or unique moments of man's life. And, like most objects, the pleasure it gives tends to be private; hence the paradox of a large architectural ensemble with an essentially private impact. This kind of aesthetic objective, which seeks to emphasize a frame and to endow it with physical beauty in such a way that the quality but not the nature of what happens within the frame is affected, was deeply imbedded in at least one side of the medieval Islamic tradition – that of the great carpets and gardens of Safavid Iran or the ceramics and metalwork of earlier times. It was certainly present in Islamic architecture too, as in the magnificent interiors of the seventeenth-century mosque of Isfahan, but almost none of its secular examples has been preserved so well as the Alhambra.

The uniqueness of the Alhambra consists, however, in more than its preservation. The effort involved in understanding its forms can lead in either of two directions. It can stimulate a fascination with its geometric and logical patterns, as was demonstrated by the implications of mathematical considerations of its ornament. But it can also cast a sort of spell, evoking real or imaginary events and emotions that find their place inside its walls. The first response, the search to define the sets of symmetry in the ornament, leads us from highly concrete details to totally abstract concepts. The second response, if it leads us to relive the mysterious yearnings of the two beautiful damsels in the Hall of the Two Sisters, to imagine the feelings of a captive princess in the Tower of the Captive, or, like Washington Irving, literally to see, on the Fountain of the Lions, the bloody remains of the murdered Abencerrajes, is to provide very concrete events to an abstract setting. That two such divergent processes of intellect and imagination can be inspired by the same monument is perhaps the Alhambra's most striking characteristic; and few monuments have ever, consciously or not, been endowed with the same quality. Perhaps it is the very abstraction of its ornament, with its principles related to fundamental formulations of physical reality, and the misleading simplicity of its compositions which make these divergent interpretations possible. For, as is the case with Escher's drawings and with modular contemporary architecture, a certain kind of abstraction almost compels interpretations derived from viewers rather than makers, and functions imposed by users rather than planners. Only the introduction of inscriptions created exceptions in a few places. But I hesitate to pursue the point too far, for it requires the discussion of theories of perception and artistic structure which have only begun to be elaborated.

Any work of art is both unique and typical, and it is only in so far as it can be envisaged in a set of traditions that its own original qualities appear. That the Alhambra belongs to many traditions and that it is also unique has, I hope, been made clear. But its most remarkable feature lies in the poignant fact that, consciously and with footnotes, two princes from a threatened and moribund dynasty of Muslim Spain put together a monument in which walk the ghosts of Harun al-Rashid, Khosro, Nero, the Queen of Sheba, and Solomon. Little is left of the great palaces of these emperors and mythical figures of the past, but they are present in the construction of Muhammad V the son of Yusuf I of the Nasrid dynasty from Granada.

BIBLIOGRAPHY

Apart from picture books and brief guide books, three kinds of studies have been devoted to the Alhambra. The first and most precious is the technical and archaeological work, carried out exclusively by Spanish scholars. Begun in the second half of the nineteenth century with the recording of inscriptions by Lafuente y Alcántara and Almagro Cardenas, this task went hand in hand with the enormous and successful job of repairing and restoring the remains. Its records were published in the archaeological chronicle of the journal *Al-Andalus* and, more recently, in the *Cuadernos de la Alhambra*. All future students owe an immense debt to the late Leopoldo Torres Balbás and his successors, Jesús Bermúdez Pareja and Francisco Prieto Moreno, who, as the most recent directors of the Alhambra Museum and as architects of the palace, have carried out and are continuing an endless succession of duly noted repairs, excavations, and simple observations bred out of daily contact with the monuments. Partial results of their immense labour have filtered through to a few general histories such as Marçais's *L'Architecture Musulmane d'Occident* and Volume IV of *Ars Hispaniae* by Torres Balbás, but these excellent books have broad aims and rarely obviate the need to consult the original archaeological chronicles in *Al-Andalus*, if not the archives of the palace itself. Furthermore, over twenty years have elapsed since these great summaries were put together, and much has changed in our knowledge of Islamic architecture and cultural history. History in general has been made more accessible by R. Arié's recent book on *L'Espagne Musulmane au temps des Nasrides* (1973), but much information and many ideas are still to be found in several works by E. Lévi-Provençal.

The second type of work consists of guide books and descriptions intended for the slow-paced and educated traveller. Such books, unfortunately in Spanish only, as Torres Balbás's *La Alhambra y el Generalife* and especially Gallego y Burín's *Guía de Granada* and *La Alhambra*, are precious manuals for the visitor's eyes and feet, providing him at every step with descriptions, appropriate texts, and guidance in appreciation. Gallego y Burín particularly has used with great effectiveness the immensely rich sources from the period which followed the reconquest of Granada, when not only could architectural or decorative details which are lost today be recorded, but it was still possible to know, to remember, or to imagine with some accuracy the life and the practices of the palace, the times when the monument was not quite yet a work of art. Just as one can walk through the Alhambra with nineteenth-century Romantic eyes, one can follow almost the same path with Renaissance Spanish eyes; the great merit of Gallego y Burín's books is that they are highly annotated cicerones reflecting the variety of ways in which Europeans have seen the Alhambra. What is missing in them is the Muslim world; and the genre of a walking meditation on a building, while essential on the spot, does not lend itself easily to historical interpretations of greater depth than an occasional judgement of value or a comparison with some well-known masterpiece.

A pitifully small number of studies have been devoted to the deeper intellectual, aesthetic, and historical questions posed by the Alhambra. One is a complicated thesis in mathematics on the principles of its decorative designs. Published in 1944 by Edith Müller, it is a very rare book and quite arcane to the non-mathematician, but it poses in unique fashion the question of geometrical ornament in set theory, a problem with wide ramifications within contemporary concerns with the arts. To the historian a far more important, in fact a revolutionary, contribution was made by Frederick Bargebuhr in an article published in 1956 and a book which appeared in 1968. Both of these studies sought to develop an iconography of the Alhambra, to search for the meanings which can be attributed to its forms. Bargebuhr's point of departure was not the fourteenth-century building but a series of discoveries in medieval Jewish and Arabic poetry of the eleventh century, and his position is that of a historian of ideas more than of art. While some of Bargebuhr's interpretations are less convincing than others, all scholars must be indebted to his discoveries and to his perception of a medieval palace in Spain, and it would not be too much to say that he has set the understanding of the Alhambra on a totally new basis. Finally some brief but extremely suggestive remarks on the gardens of the Alhambra were made by James Dickie, opening up hitherto uncharted directions for research.

This brief account clearly shows how much research is still to be done. It would be particularly valuable to have a new publication of accurate plans and elevations as well as a systematic repertory of ornament. The list which follows includes the main studies directly pertinent to the monument or to the history of the time, which could form a first orientation for its problems. Additional works as well as comparative material are found in the notes to the text.

HISTORY AND CIVILIZATION

Rachel Arié, *L'Espagne Musulmane au temps des Nasrides*, 1232–1492 (Paris, 1973).

Emilio García Gómez, *Cinco Poetas Musulmanes* (Madrid, 1944).

E. Lévi-Provençal, *L'Espagne Musulmane au Xème siècle* (Paris, 1932).

A. R. Nykl, *Hispano-Arabic Poetry* (Baltimore, 1946).

H. Pérès, *La Poésie andalouse en arabe classique au XIème siècle* (Paris, 1953).

Claudio Sánchez-Albornoz, *La España Musulmana*, Vol. II (Buenos Aires, 1960).

D. Francisco Javier Simonet, *Descripción del Reino de Granada* (new ed. Granada, 1872).

Leopoldo Torres Balbás, *Ciudades Hispano-Musulmanes* (Madrid, n.d.).

Ibn Fadl Allah al-'Umari, *Masalik*, tr. M. Gaudefroy-Demombynes (Paris, 1927).

W. Montgomery Watt and P. Cachia, *A History of Islamic Spain* (Edinburgh, 1965).

DESCRIPTIONS

Dario Cabanelas, 'La antigua policromia del techo de Comares de la Alhambra', *Al-Andalus*, Vol. XXXV (1970).

Albert F. Calvert, *Granada and the Alhambra* (London, 1907).

R. Contreras, *La Alhambra* (Madrid, 1878).

Antonio Gallego y Burín, *Granada* (Madrid, 1961).

Antonio Gallego y Burín, *La Alhambra* (Granada, 1963).

Théophile Gautier, *Voyage en Espagne* (Paris, 1843).

Jules Goury and Owen Jones, *Plans, Elevations, Sections, and Details of the Alhambra* (2 vols., London, 1842–5).

Emilio García Gómez and Jesús Bermúdez Pareja, *The Alhambra: The Royal Palace* (Florence, 1967).

Gamal Mehrez, *Las Pinturas Murales en el Partal* (Madrid, 1951).

Jesús Bermúdez Pareja, *The Alhambra: the Generalife and the Towers* (Florence, 1969).

Girault de Prangey, *Essai sur l'Architecture des Arabes* (Paris, 1841).

L. Seco de Lucena, *La Alhambra, como fué y como es* (Granada, 1935).

Leopoldo Torres Balbás, 'La Alhambra de Granada antes del siglo XIII', *Al-Andalus*, Vol. V (1940).

Leopoldo Torres Balbás, *La Alhambra y el Generalife de Granada* (Madrid, 1953).

INSCRIPTIONS

Antonio Almagro Cardenas, *Estudio sobre las Inscripciónes Arabes de Granada* (Granada, 1879).

Emilio Lafuente y Alcántara, *Inscripciónes Arabes de Granada* (Madrid, 1859).

A. R. Nykl, 'Inscripciónes árabes de la Alhambra', *Al-Andalus*, Vol. IV (1936).

Readings of inscriptions are also found in the great descriptions by Girault de Prangey and Goury and Jones.

INTERPRETATIONS AND DISCUSSIONS

Melchor Fernandez Almagro, *Granada en la Literatura Romantica Española* (Madrid, 1951).

Frederick Bargebuhr, 'The Alhambra Palace of the Eleventh Century', *Journal of the Warburg and Courtauld Institutes*, Vol. XIX (1956).

Frederick Bargebuhr, *The Alhambra, A Cycle of Studies on the Eleventh Century in Moorish Spain* (Berlin, 1968).

James Dickie, 'The Hispano-Arab Garden, its philosophy and function', *Bulletin of the School of Oriental and African Studies*, Vol. XXXI (1968).

Emilio García Gómez, *Silla del Moro* (Madrid, 1948).

Basilio Pavòn Maldonado, *Arte Toledano* (Madrid, 1973).

Georges Marçais, 'Salle, Anti-salle', *Université d'Alger, Institut d'Etudes Orientales, Annales*, Vol. X (1952).

Georges Marçais, *L'Architecture Musulmane d'Occident* (Paris, 1954).

Georges Marçais, *Mélanges d'Histoire et d'Archéologie de l'Occident Musulman* (2 vols., Algiers, 1957)

Edith Müller, *Gruppentheoretische und Strukturanalytische Untersuchungen der maurischen Ornamente aus der Alhambra in Granada* (Rüschlikon, 1944).

P. Ricard, *Pour comprendre l'Art Musulman dans l'Afrique du Nord et en Espagne* (Paris, 1924).

Desmond Stewart, *The Alhambra* (New York, 1974).

Henri Terrasse, 'Gharnātah', *Encyclopaedia of Islam* (2nd ed.; Leiden, 1954 etc.).

NOTES

Works listed in the Bibliography above are given shortened references here.

INTRODUCTION

1. Washington Irving, *A Chronicle of the Conquest of Granada* (Philadelphia, 1829), Vol. I, pp. 648 ff.
2. Quoted by Albert Champdor, *L'Alhambra de Grenade* (Paris, 1952), pp. 12–13. I have failed to find the exact original location of the quotation, but it reflects a mood about the building which can easily be demonstrated through mid-nineteenth-century French poetry.
3. Irving, op. cit., p. 14.
4. Almagro, *Granada*, p. 50.
5. Jules Goury and Owen Jones, *Plans, Elevations, Sections, and Details of the Alhambra* (1842–5); Girault de Prangey, *Essai sur l'Architecture des Arabes* (1841).

CHAPTER 1 (*pages 25–98*)

1. Quoted in Terrasse, 'Gharnătah'.
2. L. Torres Balbás, 'Esquema demografico de la ciudad de Granada', *Al-Andalus*, Vol. XXXVIII (1956); Arié, *L'Espagne Musulmane*, pp. 339 ff.
3. *Ars Hispaniae*, Vol. III (Madrid, 1959), pp. 257 ff.
4. Al-'Umari, p. 229.
5. Grabar, *The Formation of Islamic Art* (New Haven, 1973), Fig. 11.
6. Bargebuhr, *Alhambra*, pp. 89 ff.; for the main Arab source, the *Memoirs* of 'Abdallah, I used the Cairo edition, *Madhakarat al-Amīr Abdallah* (Cairo, 1955), pp. 45 and 130; see below, pp. 127–8.
7. J. Bermúdez Pareja, 'La Fuente de los Leones', *Cuadernos de la Alhambra*, Vol. III (1965), pp. 21–30.
8. Arié, *passim*; Watt, *Islamic Spain*, pp. 147 ff.
9. Torres Balbás, *Ciudades Hispano-Musulmanes*, pp. 87 ff.; Simonet, *Descripción del Reino de Granada*, pp. 43 ff.; García Gómez, *Cinco Poetas Musulmanes*, pp. 171 ff; Arié, pp. 301 ff.
10. The best attempt is by Torres Balbás, 'La Alhambra de Granada antes del siglo XIII'.
11. Nasir-i Khosro, *Sefer-nameh*, tr. Charles Schefer (Paris, 1881; repr. Amsterdam, 1970), pp. 127 ff., esp. pp. 157 ff.; Abu al-Fadl Bayhaqi,

Ta'rikh Mas'ud, tr. A. K. Arends (Tashkent, 1962), pp. 69, 267 ff., 355 ff.

12. Main texts and information in J. Lassner, *The Topography of Baghdad* (Detroit, 1970); D. Sourdel, 'Questions de Cérémonial Abbaside', *Revue des Etudes Islamiques*, Vol. XXVIII (1960).

13. List and descriptions in Seco de Lucena, *Alhambra*, pp. 85 ff.; Pareja, *Alhambra: Towers*, pp. 3 ff.

14. Arié, Fig. 3.

15. Seco de Lucena, pp. 117 ff., esp. pp. 122–4.

16. Gautier, *Voyage*, 1879 edition, p. 221.

17. Gallego y Burín, *Alhambra*, pp. 24–31; Seco de Lucena, pp. 90–93; for the inscriptions, Lafuente, pp. 85–6.

18. Gallego y Burín, *Alhambra*, pp. 180–86; Seco de Lucena, pp. 95–8.

19. Gallego y Burín, *Alhambra*, p. 168; Seco de Lucena, pp. 109–10.

20. Gallego y Burín, *Alhambra*, pp. 53–4; *Ars Hispaniae*, Vol. IV (Madrid, 1949), p. 86.

21. Gallego y Burín, *Alhambra*, pp. 35–52; M. Gomez Moreno Martinez, 'Granada en el siglo XIII', *Cuadernos de la Alhambra*, Vol. II (1966).

22. There are no detailed discussions of these sections except in guide books and general manuals. For the inscriptions see Nykl, 'Inscripciónes', pp. 176–7. The passage of Ibn Zamrak mentioned in this section is found in Sánchez-Albornoz, *España Musulmana*, Vol. II, p. 422. Marmol's texts are given in full in Gallego y Burín, *Alhambra*, pp. 65–6.

23. Gallego y Burín, *Alhambra*, pp. 68–73; Contreras, *Alhambra*, pp. 151–5; Lafuente, pp. 22–9; Nykl, 'Inscripciónes', pp. 177–8; Goury–Jones, Pl. XXIII; *Ars Hispaniae*, Vol. IV, pp. 96–8.

24. Gallego y Burín, *Alhambra*, pp. 73–95; *Ars Hispaniae*, Vol. IV, pp. 98–105; Goury–Jones, Pls. IV ff.; Cabanelas, 'La antigua policromia'; Arié, pp. 190–91.

25. Torres Balbás, *Alhambra*, p. 34; Gallego y Burín, *Alhambra*, p. 77.

26. Gallego y Burín, *Alhambra*, pp. 95–111; *Ars Hispaniae*, Vol. IV, pp. 105–9; Torres Balbás, 'La Torre del Peinador de la Reina', *Archivo Español de Arte y Arqueología*, Vol. XXI (1931); Goury–Jones, Pl. XXVI.

27. Gallego y Burín, *Alhambra*, pp. 113–47; *Ars Hispaniae*, Vol. IV, pp. 109–20; Goury–Jones, Pls. XIV, XXVIII ff.

28. Latest discussion of the paintings by Basilio Pavón Maldonado, *Arte Toledano Islamico y Mudejar* (Madrid, 1973), pp. 256–66. Ms Jerrilynn Dodds has recently completed a new study of these paintings with rather startling results which should soon appear in print.

29. Gallego y Burín, *Alhambra*, pp. 153–66; *Ars Hispaniae*, Vol. IV, pp. 120–27; for the paintings, Mehrez, *Las Pinturas*.

30. Best described in Pareja, *Alhambra*.

31. Torres Balbás, 'Paseos por la Alhambra: La Rauda', *Archivo Español de Arte y Arqueología*, Vol. VI (1926).

32. Seco de Lucena, pp. 94–5.
33. Torres Balbás, 'Crónica', *Al-Andalus*, Vols. II, X, XIV.
34. Simonet, pp. 63 ff.; Jesús Bermúdez Pareja, 'El Generalife despues del Incendio de 1958', *Cuadernos de la Alhambra*, Vol. I (1965); Torres Balbás, 'Crónica', *Al-Andalus*, Vol. IV (1939).
35. Marçais, *L'Architecture Musulmane d'Occident*, pp. 302 ff.
36. García Gómez, p. 246; Sánchez-Albornoz, *España Musulmana*, Vol. II, pp. 421–2.

CHAPTER 2 (*pages 99–157*)

1. Although this point has generally been accepted, it has never been explored and discussed in full; it permeates most of the endeavours of a pioneer scholar like Max van Berchem. See R. Ettinghausen, 'Arabic Epigraphy', in D. K. Kouymjian (ed.), *Studies in Honor of George C. Miles* (Beirut, 1974).
2. A. Bombaci, *The Kufic Inscriptions . . . of the Royal Palace of Mas'ud III* (Rome, 1966).
3. For examples and further bibliography, see O. Grabar, 'The Visual Arts', in J. A. Boyle (ed.), *The Cambridge History of Iran*, Vol. V (Cambridge, 1968). The earliest instance of poetical fragments on objects occurs on Iranian textiles of the tenth century, around the significance and authenticity of which much controversy has arisen; Gaston Wiet, *Soieries Persanes* (Cairo, 1945).
4. Poetry is used fairly commonly in seventeenth- and eighteenth-century private houses; see for instance D. Duda, *Innenarchitektur Syrischer Stadthäuser* (Beirut, 1971), pp. 136 ff.
5. María Jesús Rubiera Mata, 'Los poemas epigráficos de Ibn al-Yayyab', *Al-Andalus*, Vol. XXXV (1970). The basic study on Ibn Zamrak is by E. García Gómez, *Ibn Zamrak, el Poeta de la Alhambra* (Madrid, 1943); see also the same author's *Cinco Poetas Musulmanes*.
6. For the Muslim examples as well as for their pre-Islamic antecedents, see O. Grabar, *Formation*, pp. 141 ff.
7. A. Grabar, *Le Premier Art Chrétien* (Paris, 1966), pp. 151–3; A. Boëthius and J. B. Ward-Perkins, *Etruscan and Roman Architecture* (Harmondsworth, 1970), pp. 524 ff.
8. H. Frankfort, *The Art and Architecture of the Ancient Orient* (Harmondsworth, 1954), pp. 74–5.
9. O. Grabar, *Formation*, pp. 173 ff.
10. Ibn Hawqal, *Configuration de la Terre*, tr. J. H. Kramers and Gaston Wiet (Paris, 1964), Vol. II, p. 464.
11. For Aleppo see Jean Sauvaget, *Alep* (Paris, 1941); for Jerusalem, Max van Berchem, *Matériaux pour un Corpus Inscriptionum: Jérusalem* (Cairo, 1923).

12. K. A. C. Creswell, *The Muslim Architecture of Egypt*, Vol. I (Oxford, 1952), pp. 19 ff.
13. Ibn al-Shihna, *Les Perles Choisies*, tr. J. Sauvaget (Beirut, 1933), pp. 39 ff., among other descriptions.
14. Creswell, op. cit., Vol. II, pp. 260–64.
15. D. Schlumberger, 'Le palais ghaznévide de Lashkari Bazar', *Syria*, Vol. XXIX (1952).
16. Al-'Umari, pp. 228–30.
17. Robert W. Hamilton, *Khirbat al Mafjar* (Oxford, 1959); Richard Ettinghausen, *From Byzantium to Sassanian Iran* (Leiden, 1972).
18. M. Ecochard, *Les Bains de Damas* (Beirut, 1942–3); E. Pauty, *Les Hammams du Caire* (Cairo, 1933).
19. The reading by Nykl, 'Inscripciónes', p. 183, supersedes all earlier readings.
20. Dickie, 'The Hispano-Arab Garden'.
21. At Kish; see A. Langdon in the *Illustrated London News*, 20 February 1932, p. 273.
22. P. Grimal, *Les Jardins Romains* (Paris, 1943).
23. Hamilton, op. cit., pp. 110 ff.; A. Musil, *Kusejr Amra* (Vienna, 1907), Pl. XXIV; Martin Almagro, *Qusayr Amra* (Madrid, 1975), Pl. XVI; D. Wilber, *Persian Gardens and Garden Pavilions* (Rutland, 1962); Dickie.
24. All discussed in Marçais, *Architecture*; L. Golvin, *Recherches Archéologiques à la Qal'a des Banu Hammad* (Paris, 1965).
25. G. Deverdun, *Marrakesh* (Rabat, 1959), pp. 217 ff.; al-Makkari, *History of Dynasties in Spain*, tr. P. de Gayangos (London, 1843), Vol. I, pp. 232–9, Vol. II, p. 487; E. Lévi-Provençal, *Histoire de l'Espagne Musulmane* (Paris, 1950), Vol. II, pp. 148–9; Pérès, *Poésie Andalouse*, p. 129.
26. L. Golombek, *The Timurid Shrine at Gazur Gah* (Toronto, 1969), pp. 102 ff.
27. Dickie, following Jesús Bermúdez Pareja in *Cuadernos de la Alhambra*, Vol. I (1965).
28. K. A. C. Creswell, *Early Muslim Architecture* (2nd ed. Oxford, 1969), pp. 373 ff.; H. Stern, 'Recherches sur la mosquée al-Aqsa', *Ars Orientalis*, Vol. V (1963), Fig. 36; for a general interpretation see R. Ettinghausen, *Arab Painting* (Geneva, 1962), pp. 22 ff.
29. Rashid al-Din, *Jami al-tavarikh*, tr. A. K. Arends (Baku, 1957), Vol. III, p. 194; Donald Wilber, *The Architecture of Islamic Iran: The Ilkhanids* (Princeton, 1955), pp. 146 ff.
30. Wilber, *Gardens*; A. U. Pope and P. Ackerman, *A Survey of Persian Art* (Oxford, 1939), Vol. II, pp. 1427 ff.
31. P. Underwood, 'The Fountain of Life', *Dumbarton Oaks Papers*, Vol. V (1950); L. I. Ringbom, *Paradisus Terrestris* (Helsinki, 1958).
32. E. Lévi-Provençal, *L'Espagne Musulmane*, pp. 174–5.

33. Dickie, pp. 240–41.
34. Bargebuhr, *Alhambra*, pp. 172–7, with full bibliography; and see above, p. 34.
35. Bargebuhr, *Alhambra*, pp. 170–72.
36. Bargebuhr, *Alhambra*, pp. 149 ff.
37. Bargebuhr, *Alhambra*, pp. 97–101 and *passim*; see the review by O. Grabar in the *Art Bulletin*, Vol. LII (1970), pp. 197–200.
38. G. Vajda, 'La description du Temple', *Journal Asiatique*, Vol. CCXLVII (1959), p. 196.
39. Bargebuhr, *Alhambra*, p. 139.
40. The main references to the various accounts summarized in the text are found in A. and O. Grabar, 'L'essor des arts inspirés par les cours princières', *L'Occidente e l'Islam nell'alto Medioevo* (Spoleto, 1965); O. Grabar, *Formation*, pp. 168 ff.; O. Grabar, 'Imperial and Urban Art in Islam; the subject matter of Fatimid Art', *Colloque International sur l'Histoire du Caire* (Cairo, 1972); A. Grabar, *L'Iconoclasme Byzantin* (Paris, 1957), pp. 170 ff. It would be very useful to study these and other related texts in a more systematic manner.
41. E. Rey, *Les Colonies franques de Syrie* (Paris, 1883), p. 8.
42. F. Gabrieli, 'Il palazzo hammadita', *Festschrift für Ernst Kühnel* (Berlin, 1959); Pérès, pp. 135 ff.
43. Boëthius and Ward-Perkins, op. cit., pp. 254 ff. and 328 ff.; for the relationship to gardens, P. Grimal, op. cit., *passim*.
44. Boëthius and Ward-Perkins, op. cit., pp. 526–7; O. Grabar, *Formation*, Chapter IV.
45. Lévi-Provençal, *Histoire*, Vol. II, pp. 132 ff.; Pérès, p. 129.
46. L. Torres Balbás in *Al-Andalus*, Vol. X (1945).
47. Hamilton, op. cit., p. 34.
48. E. Lévi-Provençal, 'Notes de toponomastique hispano-magrébine', *Annales de l'Institut d'Etudes Orientales, Alger*, Vol. II (1936), esp. pp. 227 ff.
49. Almost none of these have been published; the monuments of Meshed, Herat, and Samarqand are particularly remarkable for this feature, which deserves deeper analysis.
50. The clearest statement of the question is in Marçais, *Architecture*, pp. 304–5.
51. See the references in notes 16, 17 and 26 for most of these examples.
52. Sourdel, op. cit.; M. Canard, 'Le cérémonial Fatimite et le cérémonial Byzantin', *Byzantion*, Vol. XXI (1951); O. Grabar, *Formation*, pp. 141 ff.
53. A rapid introduction to Ottoman palaces, with bibliography, is found in Fanny Davis, *The Palaces of Topkapi* (New York, 1970).
54. For Safavid palaces see Wilber, *Gardens; Survey of Persian Art*, pp. 79 ff.; G. Zander, *Travaux de Restauration de Monuments Historiques*

221

(Rome, 1968), and the contributions of G. Zander and E. Galdieri in R. Holod, *Studies on Isfahan, Iranian Studies*, Vol. VII (1974).

55. Gallego y Burín, *Alhambra*, pp. 23–4.

56. Goury–Jones, Pl. VII; Lafuente, p. 107, note *a*.

57. Nykl, 'Inscripciónes', pp. 180–81; Bargebuhr, p. 190.

58. Cabanelas.

59. There are all sorts of obstacles to establishing the exact text and translation of this poem, as with several other written sources from the Alhambra. I sought to check various readings and translations with each other, but I did not attempt to solve the complex philological questions raised about poems which have never been properly published. I relied primarily on the interpretation of E. García Gómez, *Ibn Zamrak*, pp. 69 ff. (or Sánchez-Albornoz, Vol. II, pp. 443–4), checking it with the text in Lafuente, pp. 127 ff., and Contreras, pp. 94 ff. As this study was being completed, I received James T. Monroe's *Hispano-Arabic Poetry* (Berkeley, 1975), which includes on pp. 346–65 a translation of twenty verses from the poem which is more accurate and more felicitous than mine. With Professor Monroe's kind permission, I have incorporated his translation of the verses from written sources which appear on the walls of the palace. The first two, the fifth one, and the last one are not in manuscript versions.

60. Gallego y Burín, *Alhambra*, p. 131 (probably mistranslated), and Contreras, p. 96.

61. The classic study on this is Karl Lehmann, 'The Dome of Heaven', *Art Bulletin*, Vol. XXVII (1945).

62. See especially the palace at Bougie, mentioned in note 42.

63. Bargebuhr, *Alhambra*, p. 98.

64. H. L'Orange, *Studies on the Iconography of Cosmic Kingship* (Oslo, 1953); latest observations in G. W. Cantino, 'Observations on the Domus Aurea', *Mesopotamia*, Vol. I (1966).

65. E. Herzfeld, 'Der Thron des Khosro', *Jahrbuch der Preussischen Kunstsammlungen*, Vol. XL (1921); F. Saxl, 'Frühes Christentum und spätes Heidentum', *Wiener Jahrbuch für Kunstgeschichte*, Vol. II (1923); H. L'Orange, 'Domus Aurea', *Serta Eitremiana* (Oslo, 1942); A. Alföldi, 'Die Geschichte des Throntubernakels', *La Nouvelle Clio*, Vol. X (1952). Although there is a considerable bibliography on this subject, it needs review and a systematic collation of textual information. See, for instance, the little-used reference from a Russian description of Constantinople of 1424–53 in which a dome of Heaven is described, *Itinéraires Russes en Orient*, tr. B. de Khitrowo (Geneva, 1889), Vol. I, p. 238.

66. R. W. Hamilton, 'The Sculpture of Living Forms', *Quarterly of the Department of Antiquities of Palestine*, Vol. XIV (1951), pp. 106 ff.; see R. Ettinghausen, *From Byzantium to Sassanian Iran, passim*.

67. Compare the views of Ettinghausen, *From Byzantium to Sassanian Iran*, pp. 17 ff., and Grabar, *Formation*, pp. 157 ff.
68. G. Le Strange, *Baghdad During the Caliphate* (Oxford, 1900), pp. 250 ff.
69. Bargebuhr, *Alhambra*, pp. 186–7; note 25 above.
70. I have profited a great deal from an unpublished paper on Solomon in the Iranian tradition by Professor Priscilla Soucek of the University of Michigan. I am most grateful to her for allowing me to read it.
71. Lafuente, pp. 142–3.
72. Contreras, pp. 148 ff.; Lafuente, pp. 176 ff.

CHAPTER 3 (*pages 159–201*)

1. C. Jencks and G. Baird, *Meaning in Architecture* (New York, 1969), pp. 79 ff.
2. Marçais, *Architecture*, p. 309, and 'Salle, Anti-salle'; Torres Balbás, 'Algunos aspectos', *Mélanges d'Histoire et d'Archéologie* (Algiers, 1957), Vol. II, pp. 169 ff.
3. Marçais, *Architecture*, p. 214.
4. *Excavations at Dura-Europos, Prel. Report of the Ninth Season*, Vol. III (New Haven, 1952), pp. 1 ff.
5. The basic study is by M. S. Bulatov, 'O nektoryh priemah', *Izv. Akad. Nauk Tajik SSSR*, Vol. III (1953). It has been used in the more accessible works by G. A. Pugachenkova and L. I. Rempel.
6. Marçais, *Architecture*, pp. 118 ff.
7. O. Grabar, 'La mosquée de Damas', *Synthronon* (Paris, 1968).
8. The history of this most celebrated building is now being completely re-evaluated. See E. Galdieri, *Isfahan* (Rome, 1972 and 1973); also O. Grabar, 'Notes on the Masjid-e Jomeh', *A. U. Pope Memorial Volume* (forthcoming).
9. Marçais, *Architecture*, pp. 339 ff.
10. Marçais, *Architecture*, pp. 231 and 336–7; B. Maslow, *Les Mosquées de Fez* (Paris, 1937), with excellent technical discussions.
11. There is no adequate history of the muqarnas. A few early studies, based on Egypt or Iran, are by now not very satisfactory. L. Hautecœur, 'De la trompe au muqarnas', *Gazette des Beaux Arts* (1931); J. Rosintal, *Le Réseau* (Paris, 1937); E. Pauty, 'Contribution à l'étude des stalactites', *Bull. Inst. Fr. d'Archéologie Orientale*, Vol. XXIX (1929).
12. O. Grabar, 'The Visual Arts', in R. N. Frye (ed.), *The Cambridge History of Iran*, Vol. IV (Cambridge, 1975).
13. Marçais, *Architecture*, p. 103; L. Golvin, 'Note sur quelques fragments de plâtre', *Mélanges d'Histoire à Georges Marçais* (Algiers, 1957), pp. 83 ff.
14. Goury–Jones, Pl. X.

15. H. Terrasse, *La Mosquée al-Quaraouiyin à Fès* (Paris, 1968); also in *Ars Orientalis*, Vol. II (1954).

16. G. Marçais, 'Remarques sur l'esthétique musulmane', *Mélanges d'Histoire et d'Archéologie de l'Occident Musulman*, Vol. I, pp. 99 ff.; *Architecture*, pp. 347–8.

17. F. Oelmann, 'Hilani und Liwanhaus', *Bonner Jahrbücher*, Vol. CXXVII (1922).

18. Marçais, *Architecture*, pp. 350 ff. Girault de Prangey and Goury-Jones published many details of patterns but no systematic analysis.

19. Müller, *Gruppentheoretische-Untersuchungen*. Much simpler analyses are found in Ricard, *Pour comprendre l'Art Musulman*.

20. G. Marçais, 'Nouvelles remarques sur l'esthétique musulmane', *Mélanges d'Histoire et d'Archéologie de l'Occident Musulman*, Vol. I, pp. 105 ff.

21. M. Dimand, 'Studies in Islamic Ornament', *Ars Islamica*, Vol. IV (1937), and *Archaeologia Orientalia in Memoriam E. Herzfeld* (Locust Valley, 1952); see also F. Shafi'i, *Simple Calyx Ornament* (Cairo, 1956).

22. L. I. Rempel, *Arkitekturny Ornament Uzbekistana* (Tashkent, 1961); see also N. Ardalan, *The Sense of Unity in Iranian Architecture* (Chicago, 1973).

23. Torres Balbás in *Ars Hispaniae*, Vol. IV, p. 179 and Fig. 191.

24. O. Grabar, *Formation*, pp. 188 ff.

25. Marçais, *Architecture*, pp. 352 ff; Ricard, pp. 165 ff. A complete inventory of floral elements has yet to be made.

26. For instance in the marble panels of Cordova, *Ars Hispaniae*, Vol. III, Fig. 176; Grabar, *Formation*, p. 196.

27. Müller.

28. J. Bronowski, 'The Music of the Spheres', printed in *The Listener*, 7 June 1973, and *The Ascent of Man* (London, 1973), pp. 168–76.

29. Note 22 above.

30. This is still a very obscure period; a most readable, though partly outdated, introduction is A. Mez, *The Renaissance of Islam* (English tr. Patna, 1937).

31. I. Ahrarov and L. Rempel, *Reznoi Shtuk Afrasiyaba* (Tashkent, 1971).

32. I owe many of these points to the work done on her doctoral dissertation by Miss Wasma' Chorbachi.

33. M. L. Teuber, 'Sources of Ambiguity in the Prints of Maurits C. Escher', *Scientific American*, July 1974; Bronowski, op. cit.; H. Weyl, *Symmetry* (Princeton, 1952), pp. 109–15.

34. Ardalan, op. cit.

35. Mehrez, *Las Pinturas*.

36. For further discussion see the forthcoming study by Ms Jerrilynn Dodds.

37. Terrasse, *Mosquée*, Pl. 105.

38. John Summerson, *Heavenly Mansions and other Essays on Architecture* (New York, 1963).

39. Gabriel Rousseau, *Le Mausolée des Princes Sa'adiens* (Paris, 1965).

40. Terrasse, *Mosquée*, Pl. 122.

CONCLUSION (*pages 203–10*)

1. 1898 London edition p. 151.

2. All the works from Spain are now available in Maldonado, *Arte Toledano*.

3. O. Grabar, 'The Umayyad Dome of the Rock', *Ars Orientalis*, Vol. III (1957).

4. For individual examples, see L. T. Giuzalian, 'A Bronze Qalamdan', *Ars Orientalis*, Vol. VII (1968), and 'Bronzovoi kuvshin', *Pamiatniki Epohi Rustaveli* (Leningrad, 1938); O. Grabar, 'The Inscriptions of the Madrasah-mausoleum of Qaytbay', in D. K. Kouymjian (ed.), *Studies in Honor of George C. Miles* (Beirut, 1974).

5. A. S. Melikian-Chirvani, 'Le royaume de Solomon', *Le Monde Iranien et l'Islam*, Vol. I (1971); P. Soucek, 'The influence of Persepolis', *Actes du XXIX Congrès des Orientalistes* (Paris, 1975), pp. 195 ff.

6. A. and O. Grabar, 'L'essor des arts inspirés par les cours princières', *L'Occidente e l'Islam nell'alto Medioevo* (Spoleto, 1965); O. Grabar, 'Imperial and Urban Art in Islam; the subject matter of Fatimid Art', *Colloque International sur l'Histoire du Caire* (Cairo, 1972).

7. H. L'Orange, *Studies on the Iconography of Cosmic Kingship* (Oslo, 1953).

8. O. Grabar, 'Survivances classiques dans l'art de l'Islam', *Annales Archéologiques Arabes Syriennes*, Vol. XXI (1971).

INDEX

Pages that include illustrations are given in *italic* figures

227

THE ROYAL PALACE

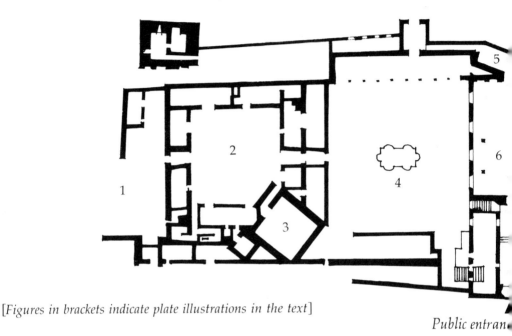

[Figures in brackets indicate plate illustrations in the text]

Public entran